STUDY GUIDE

The American West, c1835–c1895

Edexcel - GCSE

www.GCSEHistory.com

Published by Clever Lili Limited.

contact@cleverlili.com

First published 2020

ISBN 978-1-913887-41-4

Copyright notice

All rights reserved. No part of this publication may be reproduced in any form or by any means (including photocopying or storing it in any medium by electronic means and whether or not transiently or incidentally to some other use of this publication) with the written permission of the copyright owner. Applications for the copyright owner's written permission should be addressed to the publisher.

Clever Lili has made every effort to contact copyright holders for permission for the use of copyright material. We will be happy, upon notification, to rectify any errors or omissions and include any appropriate rectifications in future editions.

Cover by: Benedicte Wrensted / National Archives at College Park on Wikimedia Commons

Icons by: flaticon and freepik

Contributors: Rebecca Lawrence, Muirin Gillespie-Gallery, Emily Bishop, James George, Shahan Abu Shumel Haydar, Marcus Pailing

Edited by Paul Connolly and Rebecca Parsley

Design by Evgeni Veskov and Will Fox

All rights reserved

DISCOVER MORE OF OUR GCSE HISTORY STUDY GUIDES
GCSEHistory.com and Clever Lili

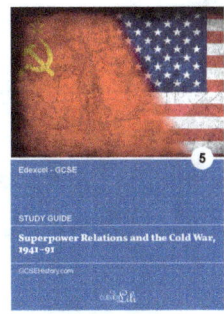
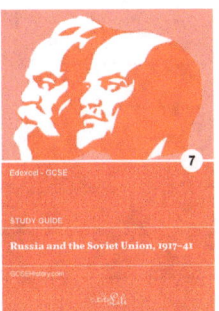
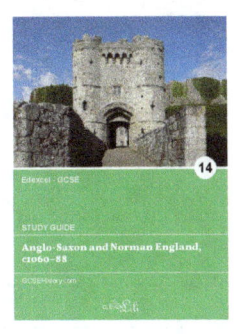

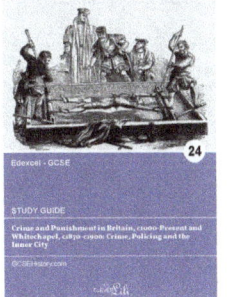

THE GUIDES ARE EVEN BETTER WITH OUR GCSE/IGCSE HISTORY WEBSITE APP AND MOBILE APP

GCSE History is a text and voice web and mobile app that allows you to easily revise for your GCSE/IGCSE exams wherever you are - it's like having your own personal GCSE history tutor. Whether you're at home or on the bus, GCSE History provides you with thousands of convenient bite-sized facts to help you pass your exams with flying colours. We cover all topics - with more than 120,000 questions - across the Edexcel, AQA and CIE exam boards.

Contents

How to use this book 6
What is this book about? 7
Revision suggestions 9

Timelines
The American West, c1835-1895 13

The Early Settlement of the West, c1835–c1862
The Great American Desert 16
Native Americans 17
The Importance of Horses 19
The Importance of the Buffalo 20
Tipis 21
The Indian Wars 21
The Indian Removal Act 22
The Permanent Indian Frontier 22
The Trail of Tears 23
The Indian Trade and Intercourse Act 23
The 1851 Indian Appropriations Act 24
The Reservation System 24
Pioneer Farmers 25
The Oregon Trail 26
Marcus Whitman 27
John Fremont 28
The California Gold Rush 28
Manifest Destiny 29
The Donner Party 29
Joseph Smith 30
The Mormon Migration 31
Brigham Young 33
The Great Plains Settlements in the 1850s 33
Scalping 34
The First Fort Laramie Treaty, 1851 35
Miners 36
San Francisco 37
Law and Order in the 1850s 38
Vigilance Committees 39

Development of the Plains, c1862-1876
The Causes of the American Civil War 40
The Homestead Act 41
The Transcontinental Railroad 42
The Pacific Railroad Act 44
Railroad Companies 45
Homesteaders 46

Daniel Halladay 47
Windmill 47
Barbed Wire 48
Sulky Plow 48
Mennonites 49
Red Turkey 49
The Timber and Culture Act 49
Hell on Wheels 50
Cow Towns 50
Abilene 51
Thomas Smith 51
Wild Bill Hickok 52
The Reno Gang 52
The Texan Cattle Industry 53
Texas Fever 53
The Quarantine Laws for Cattle 54
Joseph McCoy 54
The Chisholm Trail 55
The Goodnight-Loving Trail 55
Charles Goodnight 56
Oliver Loving 56
John Iliff 57
Cattle Trails 57
Cattle Barons 58
Cowboys 58
Cattle Ranches 59
The Peace Policy 61
Ely S Parker 61
The 1871 Indian Appropriations Act 62
Little Crow 62
The Dakota Sioux 62
Little Crow's War 63
The Fort Wise Treaty 64
Dog Soldiers 65
The Cheyenne Uprising 65
The Sand Creek Massacre 65
Colonel Chivington 66
Red Cloud's War 66
Red Cloud 67
Crazy Horse 68
Sitting Bull 68
Fetterman's Trap 68
The Second Fort Laramie Treaty, 1868 69

Conflicts and Conquest, c1876-1895

- Dry Farming 69
- The Seed Drill 70
- The Cattle Industry in the 1880s 70
- The Great Die-up 71
- The Exoduster Movement 71
- Benjamin Singleton 72
- Henry Adams 73
- The Oklahoma Land Rush 73
- Sharecroppers 74
- Billy the Kid 74
- The Lincoln County War 75
- John Chisum 76
- Murphy 76
- Pat Garrett 76
- Wyatt Earp 76
- The Johnson County War 77
- Ella Watson and Jim Averill 78
- The Wyoming Stock Growers' Association 79
- The Battle of Little Bighorn (1876) 79
- General George Armstrong Custer 81
- Wounded Knee 81
- The Ghost Dance 82
- The Dawes Act 83
- The Closure of the Frontier 84

- Glossary 85
- Index 88

HOW TO USE THIS BOOK

In this study guide, you will see a series of icons, highlighted words and page references. The key below will help you quickly establish what these mean and where to go for more information.

Icons

 WHAT questions cover the key events and themes.

 WHO questions cover the key people involved.

 WHEN questions cover the timings of key events.

 WHERE questions cover the locations of key moments.

 WHY questions cover the reasons behind key events.

 HOW questions take a closer look at the way in which events, situations and trends occur.

 IMPORTANCE questions take a closer look at the significance of events, situations, and recurrent trends and themes.

 DECISIONS questions take a closer look at choices made at events and situations during this era.

Highlighted words

Abdicate - occasionally, you will see certain words highlighted within an answer. This means that, if you need it, you'll find an explanation of the word or phrase in the glossary which starts on **page 85**.

Page references

Tudor *(p.7)* - occasionally, a certain subject within an answer is covered in more depth on a different page. If you'd like to learn more about it, you can go directly to the page indicated.

WHAT IS THIS BOOK ABOUT?

The American West c1835-c1895 period study investigates the expansion of the American West, the settlement and development of the land, and the conflicts and conquests which resulted in the establishment of the western United States. You will study the role played by key events and individuals during its development, as well as how the American West changed the lives of many. You will focus on crucial events during this period, and study the different political, economic and social changes that occurred.

Purpose
This study will enable you to understand the complexities of how the American West came to be. You will investigate themes such as settlement, religion and beliefs, nationalism, technology, farming, government, and tribal structures. This course will enable you to develop the historical skills of explanation and analysis of key events so you can demonstrate your understanding of how events are connected.

Topics
The American West c1835-c1895 is split into three key topics:

- In Topic 1 you will study the beginnings of settlement of the American West from 1835-1862. You will investigate what life was like for the Plains Indians, as well as the US government policy which helped enable mass migration by white settlers, and how this led to tension between Native Americans and those seeking to take their land.
- Topic 2 looks at the development of the American West between 1862 and 1876. You will investigate how life on the Great Plains developed, the consequences of the Civil War on the American West, and the impact of industrialisation and how it came into conflict with the lives of Native Americans. You will analyse how these developments led to conflicts, specifically Little Crow's War, the Sand Creek Massacre, and Red Cloud's War.
- Topic 3 looks at the conflicts and conquests that occurred from 1876 to 1895. You will study how tension increased during this period, as well investigating the changes in farming and the growing cattle industry. You will investigate the continuous problems of lawlessness, and how difficult it was to establish law and order. You will focus on some significant figures, the growth of settlement (such as the Exoduster movement), and the continuous destruction of the Plains Indians' way of life and their near-extinction.

Key Individuals
Some of the key individuals studied on this course include:

- Brigham Young.
- Little Crow.
- Red Cloud.
- Abraham Lincoln.
- Crazy Horse.
- Sitting Bull.
- George Armstrong Custer.
- President Grant.

Key Events
Some of the key events you will study on this course include:

- The Californian Gold Rush.
- The American Civil War.
- Little Crow's War.
- The Sand Creek Massacre.
- The Great Sioux War.
- The Fetterman Trap.
- The Exoduster Movement.
- The Battle of Little Bighorn.
- The Wounded Knee Massacre.
- The Closure of the Frontier by the US Government.

WHAT IS THIS BOOK ABOUT?

Assessment

The American West c1835-1895 period study forms part of Paper 2, which you will have a total of 1 hour 45 minutes to complete. You should spend approximately 50 minutes on this section. There will be 3 exam questions which will assess what you have learned on The American West. c1835-1895. For Question 3, you will select two out of three options.

- Question 1 is worth 8 marks and requires you to identify two consequences of an event. You will need to support the identified consequences with facts and explain how the consequences occurred.

- Question 2 is worth 8 marks and requires you to write an analytical narrative account of an event or time period. You will need to describe what happened, as well as explain how and why events are connected.

- Question 3 is worth 8 marks and requires you to explain the importance of two events, people or developments in relation to specific situations. You will need to explain what difference the event made to the specific situation.

REVISION SUGGESTIONS

Revision! A dreaded word. Everyone knows it's coming, everyone knows how much it helps with your exam performance, and everyone struggles to get started! We know you want to do the best you can in your GCSEs, but schools aren't always clear on the best way to revise. This can leave students wondering:

- ✓ How should I plan my revision time?
- ✓ How can I beat procrastination?
- ✓ What methods should I use? Flash cards? Re-reading my notes? Highlighting?

Luckily, you no longer need to guess at the answers. Education researchers have looked at all the available revision studies, and the jury is in. They've come up with some key pointers on the best ways to revise, as well as some thoughts on popular revision methods that aren't so helpful. The next few pages will help you understand what we know about the best revision methods.

How can I beat procrastination?

This is an age-old question, and it applies to adults as well! Have a look at our top three tips below.

⚙ Reward yourself

When we think a task we have to do is going to be boring, hard or uncomfortable, we often put if off and do something more 'fun' instead. But we often don't really enjoy the 'fun' activity because we feel guilty about avoiding what we should be doing. Instead, get your work done and promise yourself a reward after you complete it. Whatever treat you choose will seem all the sweeter, and you'll feel proud for doing something you found difficult. Just do it!

⚙ Just do it!

We tend to procrastinate when we think the task we have to do is going to be difficult or dull. The funny thing is, the most uncomfortable part is usually making ourselves sit down and start it in the first place. Once you begin, it's usually not nearly as bad as you anticipated.

⚙ Pomodoro technique

The pomodoro technique helps you trick your brain by telling it you only have to focus for a short time. Set a timer for 20 minutes and focus that whole period on your revision. Turn off your phone, clear your desk, and work. At the end of the 20 minutes, you get to take a break for five. Then, do another 20 minutes. You'll usually find your rhythm and it becomes easier to carry on because it's only for a short, defined chunk of time.

Spaced practice

We tend to arrange our revision into big blocks. For example, you might tell yourself: "This week I'll do all my revision for the Cold War, then next week I'll do the Medicine Through Time unit."

Get our free app at GCSEHistory.com

REVISION SUGGESTIONS

This is called **massed practice**, because all revision for a single topic is done as one big mass.

But there's a better way! Try **spaced practice** instead. Instead of putting all revision sessions for one topic into a single block, space them out. See the example below for how it works.

This means planning ahead, rather than leaving revision to the last minute - but the evidence strongly suggests it's worth it. You'll remember much more from your revision if you use **spaced practice** rather than organising it into big blocks. Whichever method you choose, though, remember to reward yourself with breaks.

Spaced practice (more effective):

week 1	week 2	week 3	week 4
Topic 1	Topic 1	Topic 1	Topic 1
Topic 2	Topic 2	Topic 2	Topic 2
Topic 3	Topic 3	Topic 3	Topic 3
Topic 4	Topic 4	Topic 4	Topic 4

Massed practice (less effective)

week 1	week 2	week 3	week 4
Topic 1	Topic 2	Topic 3	Topic 4

REVISION SUGGESTIONS

What methods should I use to revise?

Self-testing/flash cards

Self explanation/mind-mapping

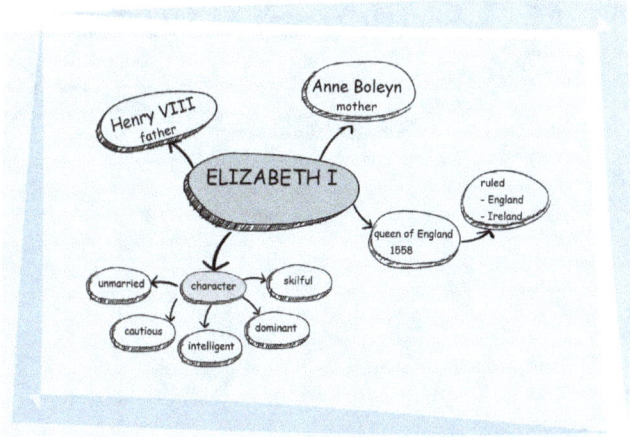

The research shows a clear winner for revision methods - **self-testing**. A good way to do this is with flash cards. Flash cards are really useful for helping you recall short – but important – pieces of information, like names and dates.

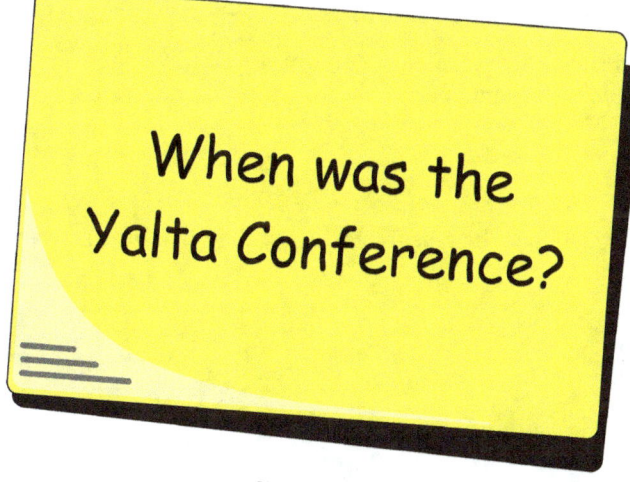

Side A - question

Side B - answer

Write questions on one side of the cards, and the answers on the back. This makes answering the questions and then testing yourself easy. Put all the cards you get right in a pile to one side, and only repeat the test with the ones you got wrong - this will force you to work on your weaker areas.

pile with right answers

pile with wrong answers

As this book has a quiz question structure itself, you can use it for this technique.

Another good revision method is **self-explanation**. This is where you explain how and why one piece of information from your course linked with another piece.

This can be done with **mind-maps**, where you draw the links and then write explanations for how they connect. For example, President Truman is connected with anti-communism because of the Truman Doctrine.

REVISION SUGGESTIONS

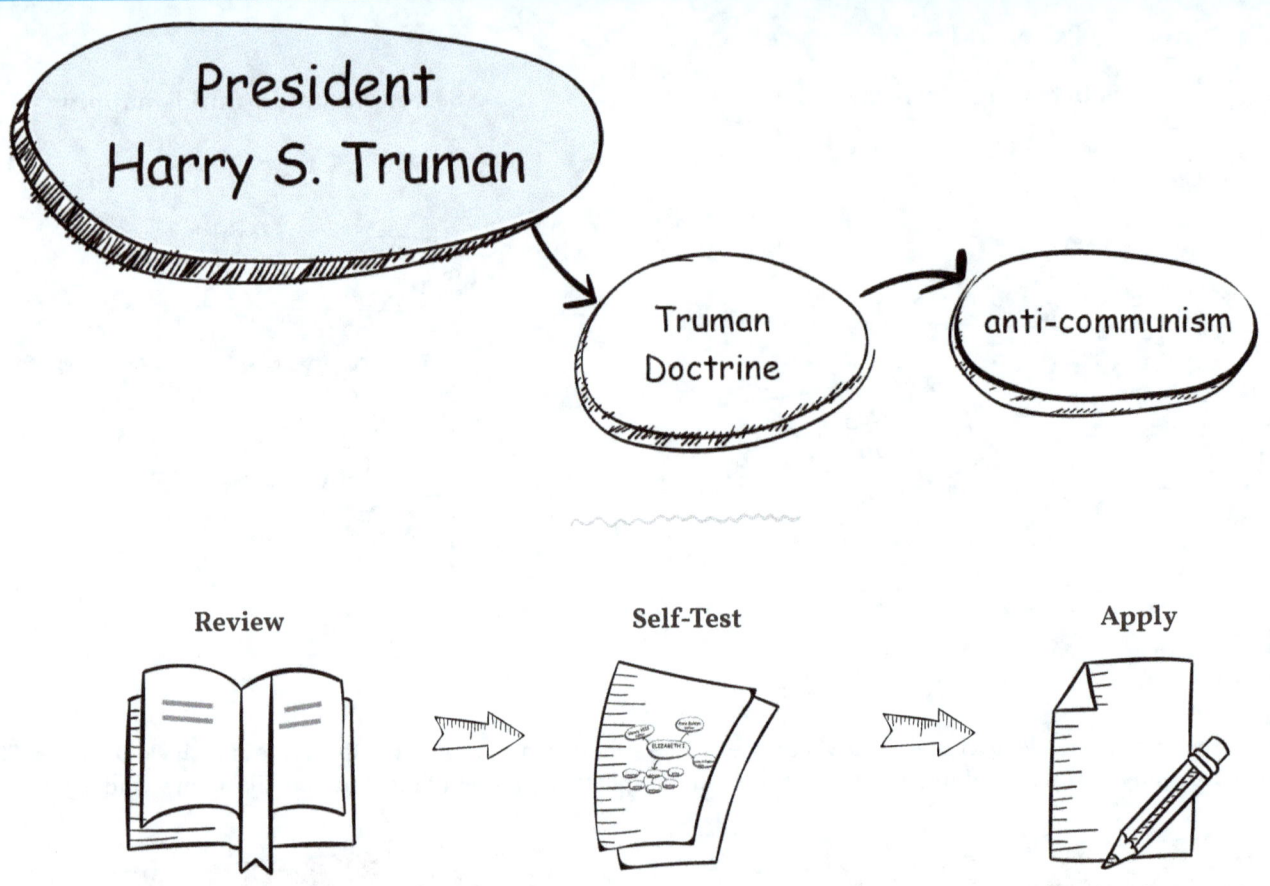

Start by highlighting or re-reading to create your flashcards for self-testing.

Test yourself with flash cards. Make mind maps to explain the concepts.

Apply your knowledge on practice exam questions.

Which revision techniques should I be cautious about?

Highlighting and **re-reading** are not necessarily bad strategies - but the research does say they're less effective than flash cards and mind-maps.

If you do use these methods, make sure they are **the first step to creating flash cards**. Really engage with the material as you go, rather than switching to autopilot.

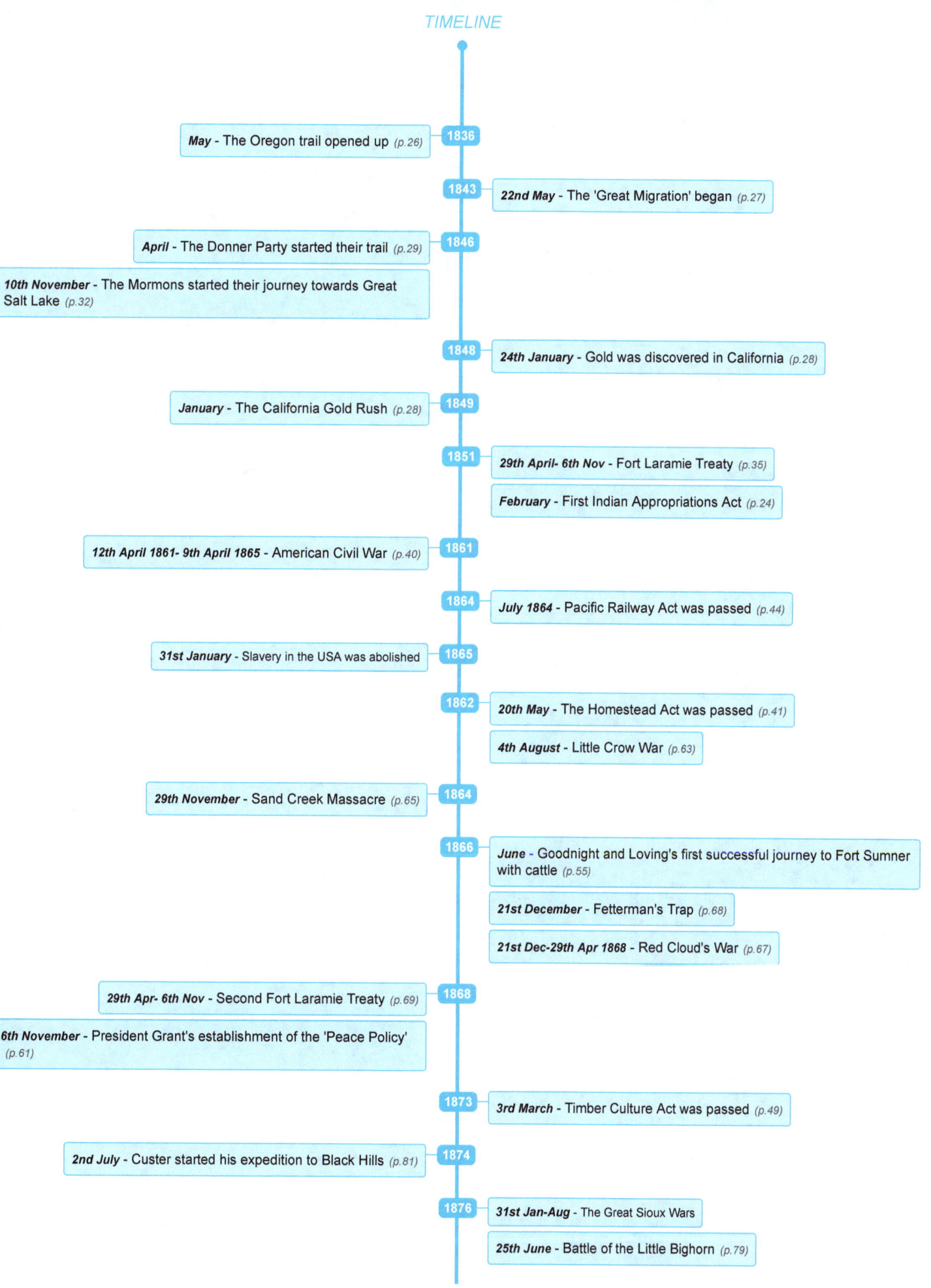

THE AMERICAN WEST, C1835-1895

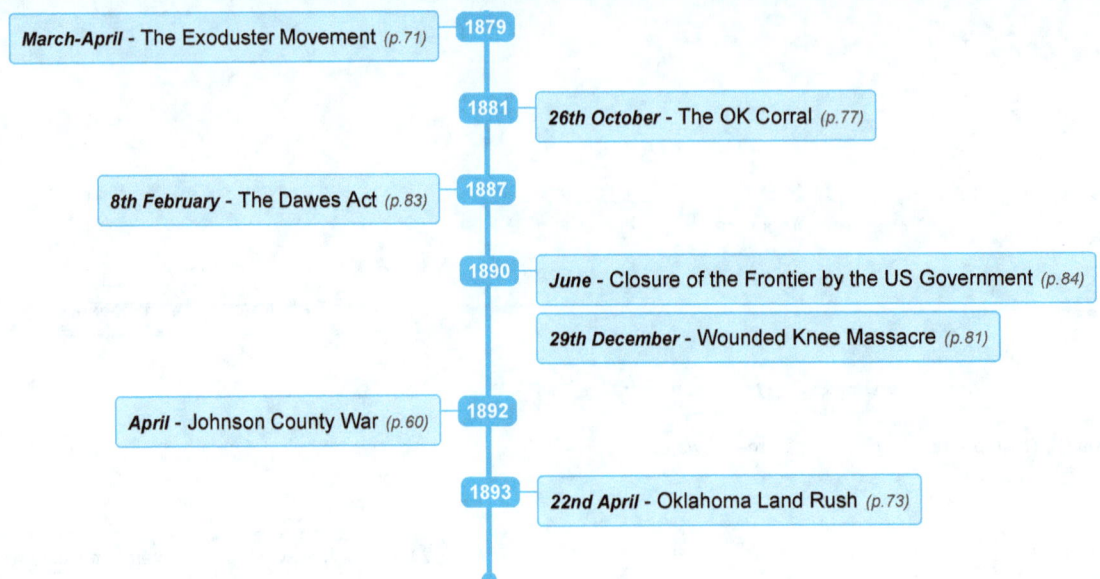

- **1879** — *March-April* - The Exoduster Movement (p.71)
- **1881** — *26th October* - The OK Corral (p.77)
- **1887** — *8th February* - The Dawes Act (p.83)
- **1890** — *June* - Closure of the Frontier by the US Government (p.84)
- **1890** — *29th December* - Wounded Knee Massacre (p.81)
- **1892** — *April* - Johnson County War (p.60)
- **1893** — *22nd April* - Oklahoma Land Rush (p.73)

THE AMERICAN WEST, C1835-1895

THE GREAT AMERICAN DESERT

The term used by people who lived east of the Mississippi River, when it was 'unknown' land.

What was the Great American Desert?
The Great American Desert was the area of land between the Mississippi River and the Rocky Mountains. This was the name given to the area by the early settlers in America - later it became known as the 'Great Plains'.

What did white settlers think of the Great American Desert?
Due to the poor conditions, the area now known as the Great Plains was dismissed by most Americans as inhospitable. They called it the Great American Desert.

Why was the Great American Desert inhospitable?
There were 3 reasons why the Great American Desert was thought to be difficult to live in.
- ☑ The weather was extreme. It was cold and windy in the winter, and hot and dry in the summer.
- ☑ A lack of natural resources, particularly wood, made it difficult to build a home or farm the land.
- ☑ Dangerous or disruptive animals, like wolves and locusts, could cause problems for settlers.
- ☑ There were huge thunderstorms. Lightning could ignite fires that raged through the dry grass.

How did native people survive in the American Desert?
Although white Americans struggled to survive on the Great Plains, Native Americans *(p.17)* thrived. They had developed ways in which to survive its conditions, mainly focused on a nomadic way of life.
- ☑ The Native Americans *(p.17)* followed the vast herds of buffalo *(p.20)*, which provided them with food and other resources. No part of a buffalo was wasted.
- ☑ They used tipis as homes, as these were easy to carry, and to erect and dismantle.
- ☑ They treated the land and animals with respect. This reverence helped them survive, as they co-existed with nature, and this honoured the Great Spirit.

How could native people survive the winter in the American Desert?
When the winter was particularly harsh the tribes sometimes moved into wooden lodges. These were circular buildings built from earth and logs, with a fire in the centre. They could fit around 60 people inside a lodge.

Why did attitudes towards the American Desert begin to change in the 1840s?
The USA won a war against Mexico in 1848. It took over land in California and Oregon. Texas also joined the Union in 1845. These two events meant that white settlers had to cross the American Desert to get to the new territories.

DID YOU KNOW?

At the time it was known as 'The Great American Desert', the area was inhabited by Native American Indians. White settlers deemed it to be uninhabitable.

NATIVE AMERICANS

The term used for the peoples who lived in America before it was taken over by white settlers.

Who were the Native Americans?
Native Americans were the first peoples to live on the American continent. They were already living diverse, successful lives when the first Europeans arrived in the seventeenth century.

How many Native American tribes were there?
There were over 500 tribes. Those that lived on the Great Plains included the Sioux, the Apache, the Pawnee, and the Cheyenne.

What did Native Americans believe about the land?
The Native Americans believed the land was sacred, and often called it 'mother'. They believed it was a living thing, and they wanted to live in harmony with the land. They believed that no-one could own the land, and most tribes believed it should not be disturbed for farming.

- An example of the Native American respect for the land is the Lakota Sioux, who saw the Paha Sapa (Black Hills of South Dakota) as particularly sacred. They believed that their tribe originated in its caves.

What were some of the Native Americans' religious beliefs?
The Native Americans had some specific religious beliefs.

- They thought that spirits could guide them through 'vision quests'. Boys received a spirit animal when they reached puberty.
- They believed they could enter the spirit world by performing dances.
- Some personal items were 'charged' with spirits. Wearing these would bring luck or protection.

Why were circles important to Native Americans?
Circles were sacred to Native Americans, who believed they have spiritual significance. They believed that life moves in a circle from birth to death and they believed that circles in nature, such as the sun and moon, are important. Tribal councils sat in circles, and the tipi *(p.21)* was built into a circle, to acknowledge the importance of the shape.

What did Native Americans believe about nature?
Native Americans believed that everything in nature has a spirit, so it was important to respect nature and to live in harmony with it.

What roles did Native Americans have within the tribe?
People's roles within the tribe depended on age and gender.

- Women married, had children, looked after their families, owned and maintained the tipi *(p.21)*, and processed the buffalo *(p.20)*. They were highly respected for this vital role.
- Men hunted, and provided for their wives and children. They led the tribe and took part in tribal ceremonies. They were also in charge of fighting.
- The elderly were well looked after by their families. However, if they felt they had become a burden, they sometimes went away from the tribe voluntarily, to die from exposure.
- Children were held in very high regard and were rarely punished. They were expected to behave well and learn from their elders.

Why did Native Americans fight?
Native Americans fought other tribes for status or for hunting areas, or they raided others to steal horses. The Sioux were considered the most warlike of all the tribes.

How did Native Americans fight?
There were a number of main features of Native American warfare.
- Native Americans would attack and retreat, using ambush as the main fighting tactic. Brotherhoods took this on as their main role. They would only attack if they thought they would win. If they began to lose they would run away.
- Warriors demonstrated their bravery by 'counting coup' on someone from another tribe. A warrior had to attempt to touch an enemy with a coup stick, and then get away. The most skilled could do this without the enemy or himself being injured or killed.
- If a Native American killed another warrior, he could remove the top of his scalp (p.34) and keep it as a trophy.

How were Native American tribes organised?
Tribes were organized in the folowing 5 ways.
- Each tribe was divided into 'bands' that worked together to survive.
- Each band could be as small as 20 or as large as several hundred people.
- Each summer, many bands might meet at a tribal gathering.
- Comanches met as a tribe a lot. Members could move between bands if they wished, as often as they wished.
- The Pawnee considered each band to be a separate village.

What was the biggest Native American tribe?
The Sioux was the largest tribe. It contained the sub-tribes of the Lakota, the Nakota and the Dakotas. The Lakota was so large it also had sub-tribes within it.

Who was the leader of a band in Native American tribes?
The most popular, most powerful and most successful members of a band were elected as the band's chief. A tribe could have lots of chiefs, each with a different role.

What were the different leaders of a band in the Native American tribes?
Depending on the needs of the tribe, they would have more or fewer chiefs. There were 3 popular types of leaders in a band.
- The War Chief.
- The Spiritual Chief.
- The Negotiation Chief, dealing with negotiations with other tribes.

How was the chief of a band chosen in the Native American tribes?
In Native American culture, reputation and power were typically gained with hunting or combat skills, and those who had gained a reputation could be chosen as chiefs.

What was the band chief's main responsibility in the Native American tribes?
A chief's main role was to make decisions for the band - usually on where they should move to, and where they should set up camp. Often the band had a council to make decisions, which was led by the chief.

What was the role of band elders in a Native American tribe?
Elders were wise people, who taught the culture and values in of the society to the younger members of the tribe, in order for their traditions and practices to continue.

What was the role of the band's council in Native American tribes?
The band's council would advise the chief in order to help him make decisions.

What are the names of some famous Native American chiefs?
Chiefs gained fame usually through wars with White Americans. Examples of famous chiefs are:
- Red Cloud *(p.66)*.
- Sitting Bull.
- Crazy Horse *(p.68)*.

What were brotherhoods in Native American culture?
Brotherhoods were an important part of Native American tribal culture.
- Brotherhoods were groups of men from the tribe or band. There could be many brotherhoods within the tribe or group.
- Members of brotherhoods taught the skills of warfare to the younger members of the tribe. They also helped with the buffalo *(p.20)* hunts.
- Men could only join a brotherhood if they had proven themselves brave and skillful warriors.
- Examples of brotherhoods in the Lakota Sioux included the Crow Owners, the White Horse *(p.19)* Riders, and the Strong Hearts.

DID YOU KNOW?

Native Americans made many great inventions. These included:
- ✔ Bunk beds.
- ✔ chewing gum.
- ✔ lacrosse.
- ✔ kayaks.
- ✔ toboggans.
- ✔ hockey.

THE IMPORTANCE OF HORSES
The Native Americans' use of horses.

What was the importance of horses to Native American tribes?
Horses were essential to the Plains tribes *(p.17)*, because they helped them move around and hunt buffalo *(p.20)*. Horses also demonstrated wealth and status.

How many horses might a Native American tribe have?
The number of horses a tribe had varied. They were a symbol of wealth, and were used as currency.

- In the 1870s, the Comanche had almost 8,000 horses, and 3,000 people.
- In the 1870s the Hunkpapa, one of the sub-tribes of the Sioux, had 3,500 horses and 2,900 people.

THE IMPORTANCE OF THE BUFFALO
Buffalo were vital to the Native Americans' survival.

What is a buffalo?
A buffalo, or bison, is a large cow-like animal, native to North America.

Why were the buffalo important to the Native Americans?
The Native Americans *(p.17)* relied on the buffalo to support their nomadic lifestyle in many ways. They were used for food, but also for clothes, utensils, and a multitude of other uses.

How did Plains Indians use the various parts of the buffalo?
There were many uses of the buffalo.
- Buffalo skin (or hide) was used for tipi *(p.21)* covers, shields, clothing, and shoes.
- The flesh of the buffalo was eaten.
- Buffalo fat was used for soap.
- Buffalo dung was used as fuel, and was smoked in ceremonies.
- Glue was made from the hooves of buffalo.
- Bowstrings were made from the sinews.
- The bones of buffalo were made into knives, jewellery, weapons, and toys.
- Buffalo horn was turned into cups and spoons.
- Buffalo tongue was used as a hairbrush.
- The fur of the buffalo was used for blankets, gloves, and padding for saddles.

Why did the buffalo almost become extinct?
After the Civil War, ex-soldiers and other white people went onto the Plains to shoot buffalo for sport. Numbers dropped so low that Native Americans *(p.17)* could no longer sustain themselves, and were forced to live on reservations. By 1890 the buffalo had almost been hunted to extinction.

Why were the buffalo respected?
The many uses of the buffalo, combined with the Native American *(p.17)* belief that all is sacred, meant that the buffalos were revered. This deep respect meant the Native Americans never wasted the buffalo, and used every part of them they could.

DID YOU KNOW?

The heart of the buffalo was never used by the Native Americans. Instead, it was left on the plains to give new life to the herd.

TIPIS
The tipi was a mobile home.

What is a tipi?
A tipi is a shelter that nomadic Native Americans *(p.17)* lived in.

What were tipis made from?
A tipi was made from buffalo *(p.20)* hide, or skin.

Why did Plains Indians live in tipis?
Tipis were simple, which was important given the general lack of resources on the Plains. They helped the Plains Indians *(p.17)* continue their nomadic lifestyle, as they were easy to put up, take down, and transport. They were also suited to the changeable weather on the Plains.

How were tipis suited to the Plains?
Tipis were conical, so harsh winds could blow around them. They had a flap for opening in the summer, to let cool air in. This could be closed in the winter, to keep warmth inside the tipi.

Who owned the tipis?
The women owned and maintained the tipi.

THE INDIAN WARS
A series of wars between Native Americans and white settlers who were trying to take their land.

What were the Indian Wars?
The Indian Wars were a series of battles and massacres between Native American *(p.17)* tribes, settlers, and government agents.

What caused the Indian Wars?
There were several reasons for the Indian Wars.

- Attitudes to land. The Native Americans *(p.17)* didn't believe land could be owned, but laws such as the Homestead Act *(p.41)* encouraged settlers to rush onto the Plains to claim land. The belief in Manifest Destiny strengthened the settlers' belief that the land was theirs to cultivate.
- Attitudes to treaties. Native Americans *(p.17)* within tribes didn't individually agree to the treaties made with the US government. Treaties were frequently broken as a result, as Native Americans strayed off their land.
- Poor conditions in the reservations. Native Americans *(p.17)* were not treated well in many of the reservations. Food was often scarce, and the Native Americans starved to death on some reservations. This led to disagreements, which sometimes turned violent.
- Broken agreements. White settlers continued to cross Native American *(p.17)* land, and even mined it. The government often did not pay compensation, which led to hostilities.
- Buffalo *(p.20)*. In the 1870s, the vast buffalo herds on the Plains were hunted almost to extinction by white hunters, who sold the hides but left the carcasses to rot. The grazing lands were also taken over by the cattle industry *(p.53)*. The elimination of their main food supply brought the Sioux into armed conflict with the military.

- ☑ The introduction of the railroad. This displaced many Native Americans *(p.17)*. It also disrupted the buffalo *(p.20)* herds.

What were the consequences of the Indian Wars?

There were 4 consequences of the Indian Wars.

- ☑ The American army destroyed Native American *(p.17)* property and resources.
- ☑ The Native American *(p.17)* population was reduced, due to starvation, fighting and disease.
- ☑ Relationships between the Native Americans *(p.17)* and the settlers worsened.
- ☑ Native Americans *(p.17)* were put onto smaller reservations, which had very poor quality land.

> **DID YOU KNOW?**
> The Indian Wars are sometimes referred to as the American Frontier Wars.

THE INDIAN REMOVAL ACT

An Act which gave President Andrew Jackson complete control over the removal of Native American tribes to make room for white settlers.

What was the Indian Removal Act?

The Indian Removal Act brought Native Americans *(p.17)* under the control of the United States. It forced those living east of the Mississippi River to move west beyond the Permanent Indian Frontier *(p.22)*, so they could live separate lives. This meant moving 46,000 Native Americans.

Who signed the Indian Removal Act?

President Jackson signed the Indian Removal Act.

When was the Indian Removal Act signed?

The Indian Removal Act was signed in 1830.

THE PERMANENT INDIAN FRONTIER

This created a boundary between the United States and Indian Territory.

What was the Permanent Indian Frontier?

The Permanent Indian Frontier was a border along the Mississippi River, dividing the eastern United States from what became known as 'Indian Territory'.

When was the Permanent Indian Frontier created?

The Permanent Indian Frontier existed from 1834.

> **DID YOU KNOW?**
>
> Indian territory got increasingly smaller, and eventually became the state of Oklahoma.

THE TRAIL OF TEARS

The forced migration of tribes from the east, which resulted in horror and sadness.

What was the Trail of Tears?

The Trail of Tears was the forced removal of eastern tribes to land west of the Mississippi River in the 1830s, under the terms of the Indian Removal Act *(p.22)*. Many Native Americans *(p.17)* died on the journey.

THE INDIAN TRADE AND INTERCOURSE ACT

An act to keep white settlers and Native Americans apart.

What was the Indian Trade and Intercourse Act?

The Indian Trade and Intercourse Act established the Permanent Indian Frontier *(p.22)*. It stated that all land west of the Mississippi River - but not in the states of Missouri, Louisiana or Arkansas - was 'Indian Territory'.

Why was the Indian Trade and Intercourse Act passed?

The Indian Trade and Intercourse Act was designed to keep white Americans and Native Americans *(p.17)* apart.

How were white Americans affected by the Indian Trade and Intercourse Act?

The Indian Trade and Intercourse Act made it illegal for any white Americans to settle on the land west of the Indian Frontier. It also made it illegal to sell weapons or alcohol to the Native Americans *(p.17)*.

How was the Indian Trade and Intercourse Act enforced?

To enforce the Indian Trade and Intercourse Act, white Americans built a military road and forts along the edge of the Indian Frontier. The forts were manned by the US Army.

> **DID YOU KNOW?**
>
> Native Americans were unable to leave their land without permission. This was another way in which they were controlled.

THE 1851 INDIAN APPROPRIATIONS ACT
The beginning of reservations.

What was the First Indian Appropriations Act?
The American government passed the First Indian Appropriations Act to provide money to move Native Americans *(p.17)* from the Indian Territory to reservations. It also allocated them land to hunt.

When was the first Indian Appropriations Act passed?
The Indian Appropriations Act was passed in 1851.

Why was the first Indian Appropriations Act passed?
The US Government wanted to move the Native Americans *(p.17)* away from white settlers. The Act created reservations, to encourage Native Americans to abandon their nomadic lifestyle in favour of farming.

> **DID YOU KNOW?**
>
> **The government hoped Native Americans would turn to farming.**
> The Act reduced the amount of land available for hunting buffalo. The government hoped this would make Native Americans want to farm, and that they would adopt the ways of white Americans.

THE RESERVATION SYSTEM
Reservations were set up so white settlers could take over Native American land.

What is a reservation?
A reservation is a fenced off area of land, where the Native Americans *(p.17)* were forced to live in order to make way for westward expansion.

What was life like on the reservations?
Life on the majority of reservations was hard, and the Native Americans *(p.17)* were often neglected by those who were supposed to care for them. Native Americans were expected to live life as white Americans did, ignoring their own culture and heritage. If they refused, rations were stopped.

Why did the Native Americans move to the reservations?
There were several reasons why the Native Americans *(p.17)* agreed to move onto reservations.
- ☑ The US Government made it sound as if the move was to protect them, and that they would be looked after.
- ☑ Many tribes were struggling to survive, as a result of having less land, less food, and more disease.
- ☑ They thought that moving to the reservations would mean that they could continue their way of life and customs in peace.

What happened if the Native Americans did not want to move to the reservations?
If the Native Americans *(p.17)* tribes refused to move to the reservations, they were forced by the US Army.

Why did the US government want the reservations?
The US government wanted to try and separate the Native Americans *(p.17)* and white Americans. They hoped this would reduce the tensions between them. They also wanted to try and 'Americanise' the Native Americans, converting them to Christianity and teaching them to become farmers.

What problems came from the reservations?
The reservations caused many problems for the Native Americans *(p.17)*.
- ☑ Chiefs often agreed to treaties which they could not enforce on their tribes, as they did not have the authority to do so.
- ☑ Some reservations were situated far from sacred places that the Native Americans *(p.17)* wanted to visit.
- ☑ Some rival tribes were placed together on the same reservations, which caused its own issues. For example, the Apache and the Navajo were placed together.
- ☑ The land in the reservations was often poor quality, even for those who did attempt to farm. This meant that the Native Americans *(p.17)* were even more dependent on the government for supplies.
- ☑ The Bureau of Indian Affairs managed the reservations, but their officials were often corrupt.
- ☑ The government often reduced the size of the reservations after pressure from white Americans, who said that it was unfair that the Native Americans *(p.17)* had so much land.

> **DID YOU KNOW?**
>
> **Life on a reservation was difficult.**
> The Native Americans on the reservations suffered problems of infant mortality, low life expectancy, poor nutrition, poverty, and alcohol and drug abuse.

PIONEER FARMERS
A pioneer farmer could get rich.

Who were the pioneer farmers?
Pioneer farmers were the first farmers to travel west, to Oregon and California.

When did the pioneer farmers go west?
People travelled west from the 1830s. They are known as the pioneer farmers.

Why did the pioneer farmers go west?
The pioneer farmers travelled west for 4 main reasons.
- ☑ They wanted independence.
- ☑ There was a financial crisis in the eastern states, which in 1837 led to 25% unemployment. Wages were cut by 40%.
- ☑ The east was becoming overpopulated.
- ☑ There was cheap farming land to claim, giving the pioneers a home and employment.
- ☑ There was a huge demand for food, so they could make a lot of money through farming, and by exporting any excess to Europe.

How did the pioneer farmers farm?
Larger farms could use steam-powered machinery, and retain a larger labour force of people.

> **DID YOU KNOW?**
>
> Some farmers could improve the land they bought, then sell it for far more than they paid for it. They then moved further west, bought more land, and repeated the process.

THE OREGON TRAIL
A trail that was established to encourage settlers to move west.

What was the Oregon Trail?
The Oregon Trail was the route used by thousands of people to cross from the east, over the Great Plains, to the west. It was 3,200km long.

Where was the Oregon Trail?
The trail started in Independence, Missouri, and finished in Oregon City.

How did people travel on the Oregon Trail?
Pioneers travelled along the Oregon Trail by foot, horseback, or with wagons. They had to bring enough food for the entire journey, as well as the things they needed for their new life. Wagons were often pulled by oxen as they were strong, but they were very slow.

Why did people travel the Oregon Trail?
People wanted to move west, as they had heard of rich farming lands which they could obtain for free. The economic conditions in the east were not good, so people saw it as a new opportunity.

At what time of year did people travel the Oregon Trail?
People were advised not to travel the Oregon Trail in winter, as it froze, and not to travel until April at the earliest. This would allow the grass to grow, so that their animals could graze along the route.

Why did settlers not use an alternative to the Oregon Trail?
People could travel by sea to Oregon, but it was extremely expensive. Each journey cost $300, and the journey could take a year. Taking the overland trail cost them the price of a wagon and supplies.

Who established the Oregon Trail?
Jedediah Smith established the Oregon Trail in 1825, when he discovered the South Pass through the Rocky Mountains.

Who were the first migrants with a wagon to use the Oregon Trail?
In 1836, two couples were the first to travel the Oregon Trail with a covered wagon for purposes other than trade. Narcissa and Marcus Whitman *(p.27)*, and Henry and Eliza Spalding, were Christian missionaries.

What other examples of people travelling the Oregon Trail are there?
Once it was open, many groups used the Oregon Trail. It was safer to travel in groups with a range of skills. They formed 'wagon trains'.
- In 1840, the Walker family travelled the trail, with their 5 children.
- A group of 60 completed the trail in 1841, and another 100 in 1842.
- The 'Great Emigration' of 1843 saw Marcus Whitman *(p.27)* leading 900 people along the trail.
- By 1846, an estimated 5,000 people had used the Oregon Trail to migrate west.

How did the government help people use the Oregon Trail?
The American government wanted people to use the Oregon Trail and move west, so they spent money on mapping and publishing reports on the trail. In 1841 the government spent $30,000 on promoting the trail.

What problems were there using the Oregon Trail?
There were many difficulties in travelling the Oregon Trail, and it is believed that around 20,000 people died on the trail, including the famous Donner Party *(p.29)*. The main problems were:
- Getting stuck.
- Drowning while crossing rivers.
- Accidents with wagons.
- Illness and disease, such as cholera.
- Running out of supplies.
- Fear of attack from Native Americans *(p.17)*, although there are no recorded accounts of any.
- The length of the journey. The average journey on the Oregon Trail took four months.

> **DID YOU KNOW?**
> **The trail was full of litter!**
> Many travellers would dump old wagons, clothes, food, and other rubbish.

MARCUS WHITMAN
The first migrant to cross the Oregon Trail. Later he led the 'Great Emigration'.

Who was Marcus Whitman?
Marcus Whitman was one of the first people to cross the Oregon Trail *(p.26)* as a migrant rather than a trader. He led 900 people across the trail in 1843, calling it the 'Great Emigration'.

JOHN FREMONT
A leader on the Oregon Trail.

Who was John Fremont?
John Fremont led an expedition across the Oregon Trail *(p.26)* to map it, funded by the American government. He then published a report people could use as a guidebook. Fremont believed in Manifest Destiny.

THE CALIFORNIA GOLD RUSH
The miners would scoop up the sand, rock and gravel and mix it with water to find precious metals, hoping for gold.

What was the California Gold Rush?
The California Gold Rush refers to the time when a huge wave of prospectors moved to California, to mine for gold.

When was the California Gold Rush?
Gold was first discovered in California in 1848. The California Gold Rush started in 1849.

Who discovered gold in California that started the Gold Rush?
James W. Marshall was the first to discover gold, at Sutter's Fort in California.

How many miners went west for the Gold Rush?
By April 1849, over 200,000 miners had travelled west.

What were the effects of the Gold Rush?
There were 6 consequences of the California Gold Rush.
- ☑ The American economy received a boost, which solved previous economic problems.
- ☑ California grew rapidly, becoming an official state in 1850. By 1855, the population in California was over 300,000.
- ☑ Huge farms and other businesses sprang up in California, making it a wealthy state where independence and wealth could be made. Farmers even started to export excess food around the world,
- ☑ The California Gold Rush was used as proof to some that Manifest Destiny was real.
- ☑ Problems with Native Americans *(p.17)* on the trails to California increased.
- ☑ Mining camps were lawless places, where murder, claim jumping, racism, and assault were common.
- ☑ The wealth of the state was used in 1869 to pay for the first transcontinental railroad *(p.42)*.
- ☑ There were racial tensions with Chinese miners.

DID YOU KNOW?
When gold was discovered starting the California Gold Rush, around 300,000 people went there in search of their fortune from the US and abroad.

MANIFEST DESTINY
Destined to expand!

What was Manifest Destiny?
Manifest Destiny was the belief that white people had a God-given right to expand westwards, and to settle the entire continent of North America. It was also viewed by many as a mission to civilise the 'savage' Native American *(p.17)* tribes.

Who thought of the concept of Manifest Destiny?
The journalist John L. O'Sullivan coined the phrase in 1845, to encourage people to travel west.

Why was Manifest Destiny important?
Manifest Destiny was important for 6 reasons.
- It increased the size of the United States, as more people moved westward.
- Americans gained access to new resources, such as gold, which made the economy grow.
- It caused major unrest in the Native American *(p.17)* tribes.
- It opened up new land for settling, which led to laws such as the Homestead Act *(p.41)* of 1862.
- The idea that God wanted whites to settle the land made it easier for them to justify taking it from Native Americans *(p.17)*.
- It was a major 'pull' factor in the expansion west.

How did the painting 'American Progress' show Manifest Destiny?
The painting 'American Progress' from 1872 shows the American ideals of Manifest Destiny. The painting shows the many types of migrants, including farmers and miners, and it shows a female representation of 'progress' as the Americans move across to the West. It shows the introduction of telegraph poles and the railroad. The Native Americans *(p.17)*, the buffalo *(p.20)* herds, and wild animals are all being driven away by the white Americans.

> **DID YOU KNOW?**
> It was believed by many that God blessed the expansion of the American nation, and that He even demanded it.

THE DONNER PARTY
A group of pioneers had a dream to go west. They ended up facing terrible winter conditions, and had to make very difficult decisions to survive. And many didn't make it.

Who were the Donner Party?
The Donner Party were travellers from the east, on their way to California. They were led by the Donner brothers, using a new shorter trail mapped by Lansford Hastings. They became trapped in the mountains during the winter, and turned to cannibalism to survive.

When did the Donner Party travel to California?
The Donner Party started their journey in May 1846, but became trapped in the winter of 1846. The first person died on the 15th December.

How many people were in the Donner Party?

87 people left for California, but only 46 arrived.

Why did the Donner Party get stranded?

The Donner Party became stranded for several reasons.
- They left later than other pioneers that year.
- They took a new and more difficult route, which was meant to be shorter. However, it was away from the more common trails, so was harder to follow.
- The weather was poor, and the winter was particularly harsh. Snow storms trapped them in the mountains.
- Because the route was not established it had no forts where they could get supplies. There were also no established river crossings. These had to be created from scratch, which made the journey harder.

> **DID YOU KNOW?**
>
> **It was said that the survivors did not kill anyone to eat... except for two people.**
> - Two Native Americans, Luis and Salvador from the Miwok tribe, were sent to help the trapped pioneers. They eventually became trapped themselves.
> - When they had eaten the pioneers who died, it was decided that the Miwoks would be killed and eaten. They were seen as not 'really human'.

JOSEPH SMITH

Joseph Smith Jr. was the founder of Mormonism and the Latter-Day Saints movement.

Who was Joseph Smith?

Joseph Smith was the founder and leader of The Church of Jesus Christ of Latter-Day Saints, otherwise known as the Mormons *(p.31)*.

When did Joseph Smith found Mormonism?

Joseph Smith founded the Church of Jesus Christ of Latter-Day Saints in 1830.

Why did Joseph Smith found the Mormon Church?

Joseph Smith believed the angel Moroni visited him and gave him a book from God, with instructions to share it with everyone.

When did Joseph Smith die?

There were a number of attempts to imprison Smith, but he managed to avoid them. Eventually he was imprisoned and, while there, he was killed by a mob.

Why was Joseph Smith important?

Joseph Smith was important because he created a new form of Christianity. He was persuasive and charismatic, so people followed him.

> **DID YOU KNOW?**
>
> **He liked dogs!**
> He owned two dogs, one named Major and a bulldog named Baker.

THE MORMON MIGRATION

A religious group that believes in revelations made by their founder Joseph Smith, as well as traditional concepts of Christianity.

What are Mormons?
Mormons are members of the Church of Jesus Christ of Latter-Day Saints.

Why were the Mormons important?
The Mormons are an example of how people were able to successfully travel and settle in the west.

Who was the leader of the Mormons?
Joseph Smith *(p.30)* was the founder and first leader of the Mormons.

Why were the Mormons persecuted?
There are 7 reasons why the Mormons faced persecution in the east by white Americans.
- ✓ The Mormons expanded rapidly, leading people to fear they were trying to take over.
- ✓ The Mormons moved into their own communities, which made people fearful of them. In 1833, the Mormons' printing press was destroyed in Independence, Missouri.
- ✓ The Mormons had a militia group called the Danites, who clashed with non-Mormons at the Battle of Crooked River in 1838.
- ✓ There was a financial crash in the 1830s, and people blamed the Mormons.
- ✓ In Nauvoo, the Mormons announced that they practised polygamy, which was against the Christian beliefs of most Americans. Many Americans thought that this was blasphemy.
- ✓ The Mormons encouraged the freeing of slaves, which went against the beliefs of most people in the southern states. This belief saw them forced out of Missouri.
- ✓ Americans were genuinely worried that Joseph Smith *(p.30)* was trying to overthrow the United States government.

When did the Mormons go west?
Brigham Young *(p.33)* moved all of the Mormons west in 1846-1847.

Where did the Mormons travel to?
The Mormons moved west to the Great Salt Lake (now in the state of Utah).

When did the Mormons reach Salt Lake?
The Mormons reached the Great Salt Lake in July 1847.

How did the Mormons organise the journey to Salt Lake?
The president of the Mormon church, Brigham Young *(p.33)*, carefully planned the journey. It was organised in 6 main ways.
- ☑ 16,000 people were formed into groups of 100 wagons, each with a leader.
- ☑ Each member of the group had a job and a purpose.
- ☑ Young researched the journey thoroughly.
- ☑ Young ensured discipline was tight.
- ☑ Young organised the Mormons at the Camp of Israel, ensuring that they reached the previously built Winter Quarters by autumn.
- ☑ A pioneer band of 143 strong people was sent ahead to the Great Salt Lake, to clear and ready the route, and to prepare a site for settlement.

 ### What problems did the Mormons face on their journey west?
The Mormons faced 3 main problems on their journey.
- ☑ It was long - more than 1,000 miles.
- ☑ The weather was unpredictable.
- ☑ They didn't know what they'd find when they reached their destination.

 ### In what ways were the Mormons successful at Salt Lake?
The Mormons successfully settled at the Great Salt Lake. There are 8 reasons for this success.
- ☑ Their leader, Brigham Young *(p.33)*, was highly respected and a brilliant organiser.
- ☑ They used irrigation systems to divert water from the mountains into the dry land around the Great Salt Lake.
- ☑ They used sod (mud) bricks to make houses, as wood was in short supply.
- ☑ Brigham Young *(p.33)* told the Mormons that all land was owned by the Church. He shared out the land according to need, so the bigger families had more land.
- ☑ When the Mormons first arrived at the Great Salt Lake it was part of Mexico. Brigham Young *(p.33)* negotiated with the US government, who incorporated it into the United States, calling the territory Utah from 1850.
- ☑ The Mormons charged travellers for the right to cross their land, which boosted their economy.
- ☑ Settlements were carefully organised. Each family was given a different task, so that the whole area could be self-sufficient.
- ☑ They encouraged people to come to the Great Salt Lake from all around the world, by creating the Perpetual Emigrating Fund. This meant that money could be given to emigrants to pay for their journey to America.

 ### What is the significance of Salt Lake to the Mormons?
Salt Lake is the area where the Mormons settled after their journey west. It is now in the American state of Utah. Salt Lake City is the current headquarters of the Mormon Church.

DID YOU KNOW?

They have a lot of money!
Today, the Church's assets are thought to be worth more than $30 billion.

BRIGHAM YOUNG
The second president of The Church of Jesus Christ of Latter-Day Saints.

Who was Brigham Young?
Brigham Young was the president of the Church of Jesus Christ of the Latter-day Saints, or Mormons *(p.31)*, from 1844-1877.

Why is Brigham Young important?
Brigham Young was responsible for planning the Mormons *(p.31)*' journey to the Great Salt Lake *(p.32)*.

> **DID YOU KNOW?**
>
> Brigham Young founded Salt Lake City, and was the first governor of Utah Territory.

THE GREAT PLAINS SETTLEMENTS IN THE 1850S
Settlers migrated to the Great Plains for many reasons. On arrival, they realised life wouldn't be easy.

Who settled on the Great Plains in the 1850s?
Settlement on the Great Plains was encouraged by the US government, so many pioneer farmers settled there.

Where were the settlements on the Great Plains in the 1850s?
The settlements were in the new territories of Nebraska and Kansas, behind the Permanent Indian Frontier *(p.22)*.

Why were there problems in settling on the Great Plains?
There were three main problems with settling on the Great Plains:
- There were few water sources, such as rivers and streams, and half the amount of rainfall as in the east.
- Due to the lack of water there were few trees. Those that did grow were often burned by the Native Americans *(p.17)*, as this promoted grassland - which they wanted for buffalo *(p.20)*.
- The climate in the area meant the summers were very hot, and the winters very cold. There were also wild thunder and hail storms.

What did the conditions mean for settlements in the Great Plains?
Conditions on the Great Plains had 6 major consequences for the settlements:
- Crops could not grow in the dry conditions and livestock had little to drink.
- The lack of navigable waterways meant everything had to be transported by wagon.
- No timber was available for houses or fence building, nor for heating or cooking.
- Extreme weather and harsh storms destroyed some crops. Prairie fires were common and destroyed anything in their path.
- Deep-rooted grass made ploughing difficult. A 'sod' buster' was invented to help, but otherwise it had to be dug out by hand.

- Conditions were perfect for insects. Grasshoppers in particular could swarm in the area. They destroyed crops, and their droppings often polluted water supplies.

How did they overcome the problems in the settlements on the Great Plains?

Those that chose to settle on the Great Plains had to find solutions to the problems they experienced:

- They burned buffalo *(p.20)* dung after it had dried in the sun to use as fuel.
- They dug deep wells to find water. This was very expensive, but water was otherwise unavailable.
- They built houses from earth or sod. These were warm and fire-proof, but also often infested with insects. They also turned to mud in more severe thunderstorms.

What was life like in a settlement on the Great Plains?

Settlements were far apart and it could take days to travel to the next one or to a town. Many of those who lived there spoke about how lonely it was.

How did settlers feel about the Native Americans on the Great Plains?

Most settlers were scared of the Native Americans *(p.17)*. While some had more enlightened views, many had deep-rooted prejudices. They saw the Native Americans as savages who stole food and supplies and burned their trees. They feared being kidnapped to be used as slaves, or that they and their families would be scalped.

How did these settlers affect the Native Americans on the Great Plains?

The white settlers had a major impact on the Native Americans *(p.17)*. They disrupted the vital buffalo *(p.20)* hunting, either by killing buffalo for themselves or causing stampedes. The settlers' livestock ate much of the grassland, leaving the Native Americans' horses hungry.

> **DID YOU KNOW?**
>
> **The worst grasshopper outbreak was in 1874.**
> It was so bad it was seen as a 'plague'. Some 120 billion grasshoppers completely destroyed 300,000 acres of land.

SCALPING
A brutal way to prove victory.

What was 'scalping'?

Scalping was when the skin - including the hair - was cut from the top of the head. It was a sign of bravery and a victory trophy. Both Native Americans *(p.17)* and white Americans are known to have scalped their enemies.

THE FIRST FORT LARAMIE TREATY, 1851

A treaty that gave some tribes land and money, but only if they let settlers cross the plains.

What was the Fort Laramie Treaty?

The Fort Laramie Treaty gave land and money to each Plains tribe if they let settlers, travellers, and government agents cross the Plains in safety.

Why was the Fort Laramie Treaty signed?

The US Government was under pressure to protect people migrating west, as the migrants were worried about conflict with the Native Americans *(p.17)*. The Government's solution was to make an agreement with a council of different tribe leaders.

What problems were there in getting the Fort Laramie Treaty?

There were 5 main issues in arranging an agreement.

- The Council of Tribal Leaders. Gathering the leaders of each tribe was very problematic. Few tribes had an overall leader who could speak for all the bands within a tribe. Often the government chose them, which did not please the tribes.
- Inclusion. Many tribes were unrepresented. Some of those who attended the council only came for the food and gifts, and therefore did not take part in the discussions, to give their tribe's point of view.
- Boundaries. The US government wanted agreements made on borders and boundaries. However, Native Americans *(p.17)* did not view land in this way. They saw land as there for everyone, and could not see why their movements needed to be limited.
- Language. Not all tribes spoke the same language, and there were not enough translators to make sure everyone understood the proceedings. Not all the tribes could engage properly with the negotiations.
- Attitudes. Some white Americans were exterminators, and did not believe a peaceful agreement could or should be reached. Some Native Americans *(p.17)*, such as the Crow nation, felt the same.

When was the Fort Laramie Treaty signed?

The Fort Laramie Treaty was signed on 17th September 1851.

Who signed the Fort Laramie Treaty?

The Fort Laramie Treaty was agreed between the US government and Native American *(p.17)* tribal chiefs.

What was agreed in the Fort Laramie Treaty?

There were 7 main points agreed in the Fort Laramie Treaty.

- Fighting would end between Native Americans *(p.17)* and white Americans.
- Migrants could travel safely through Native American *(p.17)* lands.
- Railroad surveyors would be allowed to enter Native American *(p.17)* lands in safety.
- Road and army posts could be set up in the Native American *(p.17)* lands.
- Native American *(p.17)* tribes would have to pay compensation if they broke any of the agreement.
- The US Government agreed to protect Native Americans *(p.17)* from white Americans, and to stop white Americans from settling on Native American lands.
- Native Americans *(p.17)* were to receive an annual payment of $50,000, so long as they kept to the terms of the treaty.

How much money did the Fort Laramie Treaty give to the Native Americans?

The Native American *(p.17)* tribes received $50,000 a year, as long as the treaty was unbroken. However some tribes never received payment.

What were the consequences of the Fort Laramie Treaty?

The Fort Laramie Treaty had 3 major consequences for the Plains Indians *(p.17)*.

- ☑ It encouraged them to rely on the US government for food and money. This dependency also meant obedience.
- ☑ It gave each tribe their own land, rather than giving them the freedom to be truly nomadic. This resulted in the creation of reservations.
- ☑ It ended the principle of the Permanent Indian Frontier *(p.22)*, as white Americans later settled in Native American *(p.17)* lands, even though this broke the Fort Laramie Treaty.

> **DID YOU KNOW?**
>
> **Many tribes were unaware of the true impact of letting settlers, government agents and travellers on their land.**
> - ✓ Grants from the government took away a lot the land from the tribes.
> - ✓ It also left little space for the buffalo to graze, and there was nowhere for them to roam, which made hunting hard.

MINERS

Pioneers who wanted to get their hands on the precious metals discovered in California.

 ## Who were the miners?

Miners were pioneers who travelled west to pan for precious metals, such as gold.

 ## Why did the miners go west?

Gold was discovered at Sutter's Fort, California. This led to a rush of miners to the area in 1849 - hence their nickname, 'forty-niners'.

 ## Where did the miners come from?

Initially the miners came from the eastern states of the US but, as word spread, they came from Europe and Asia too.

 ## What was life like for miners?

Life in the mining camps was hard, with long, hot days and uncomfortable nights in temporary shelters. Many men did not make enough money to stay long and went home empty-handed.

 ## What was law and order like in the miners' camps?

The mining population grew so quickly that law and order *(p.38)* could not be introduced fast enough. This resulted in several problems:

- ☑ Californian law set out guidelines on how much land settlers could claim, and gave them the right to any gold found there. This was called 'staking a claim'. It sometimes led to 'claim jumping', where others stole claims from their rightful owners.
- ☑ Lack of regulation meant people often tricked others into staking a claim, by laying a few flakes of gold on the land. This was called 'salting a claim'. Others robbed prospectors as they came to view land.
- ☑ Widespread prostitution and the availability of alcohol led to many fights. Guns were readily available, so fights could be very dangerous.

- The gold rush *(p.28)* attracted many people from different countries, cultures, religions, and ways of life. This could lead to conflict, tensions and violence.

How did miners deal with law and order?

Mining towns needed to settle disputes, but did not have easy access to law and order *(p.38)*. As a result, they agreed their own rules, appointed a recorder to record disputes, and had their own courts and judges to dispense justice. Vigilantes were also common.

What was the impact of miners on the Native American population?

Miners, and the towns that grew up around the gold rush *(p.28)*, took land and resources from the Native Americans *(p.17)*. Their movement disturbed the buffalo *(p.20)*. The people also brought diseases the Native Americans had not experienced before, meaning they experienced high fatality rates. All this led to conflict and wars, such as Red Cloud's War *(p.66)*.

> **DID YOU KNOW?**
>
> 151,000 Chinese immigrants went to the USA in search of a better life. Some wanted to take advantage of the discovery of precious metals.
> - ✓ They became the largest non-white community from outside the USA.
> - ✓ However, they were viewed as 'competition' by other pioneers as they often worked for lower wages.
> - ✓ This led to the Chinese Exclusion Act in 1882, which meant a long period of poor treatment of Chinese and other Asian groups.

SAN FRANCISCO
A lawless land filled with opportunity for growth.

What was San Francisco like during the 1850s?

San Francisco grew rapidly in 1849, the population expanding from 1,000 to 25,000 people as people flocked there during the Gold Rush *(p.28)*. Growth continued into the 1850s as the miners moved in, funded by larger mining companies.

Why did Chinese migrants go to San Francisco in the 1850s?

There was a severe famine in China in 1852, which led to many Chinese migrants travelling to California and particularly San Francisco. Some 18,000 Chinese migrants had arrived by the end of 1852.

What problems were there in San Francisco like during the 1850s?

The lack of jobs, and the fact not enough gold was being found, led to several problems when it came to law and order *(p.38)*.

- Gangs established themselves in different areas of the city and formed rivalries with each other.

- Law enforcement was ineffective. There was so much crime, law officers could not keep up.
- Corruption among law officers was common.

- People literally got away with murder, as gangs killed their rivals in daylight. They could walk into saloons and shoot people with few consequences.

- ✅ Racism increased. Rules were made for Chinese miners only, which included not working on new claims. When Chinese migrants did make money, white Americans often robbed them, destroyed their camps, and sometimes murdered them.

> **DID YOU KNOW?**
>
> **Abandoned ships from the Gold Rush were upcycled.**
> They were made into homes, shops and banks.

LAW AND ORDER IN THE 1850S

It was very difficult to police the new lands in the west - it was a place where anything could happen.

What was law and order like in the American West?
'Lawless' is the word frequently used to describe law and order in the American West. There were systems, such as federal law, but the number of crimes committed overwhelmed the number of officers and the resources available.

How was law and order managed in the American West?
Towns could not apply to be their own state until their population was at least 60,000 people. Before that they were not permitted to have their own government, laws, or legal system. Instead, they had to follow federal law.

What did federal government provide so that law and order worked in the American West?
Federal government made the laws for each territory in the American West. It also provided the following:
- ✅ A governor.
- ✅ 3 judges to hear court cases.
- ✅ A US marshall, who could appoint deputies to assist him.

What did sheriffs do to help law and order in the American West?
Each community elected a sheriff once it reached 5,000 people. Sheriffs helped the US marshall enforce law and order. Their main role was to break up fights and prevent violence by calming disputes.

What problems were there with law and order in the American West?
The system of law and order suffered problems:
- ✅ Geography. Huge territories with remote areas places were extremely hard to manage and support. It would take officials a long time to investigate reports of trouble.
- ✅ Corruption was common, as law officers were poorly paid.
- ✅ Injustice. Lack of proper training, corruption, favouring friends and other pressures led to some officials acting unfairly and even unjustly.

How was law and order in the American West racist?
Chinese, African Americans and Native Americans *(p.17)*, were all subject to racist laws. For example:
- ✅ Chinese miners had to pay a higher rate of tax than white miners.
- ✅ Chinese, African Americans, and Native Americans *(p.17)* were banned from being witnesses in court proceedings.

> **DID YOU KNOW?**
>
> **A place called Aurora was the very definition of 'the Wild West'.**
> - ✓ The population was mostly male.
> - ✓ It numbered 200-300 people, half of whom were prostitutes.
> - ✓ There were 80 children, which did at least lead to a small school being built.

VIGILANCE COMMITTEES
Without the law, they became the law.

What were vigilantes in the American West?
Vigilantes were citizens who took the law into their own hands. They acted independently of the law, using their own enforcers, judges and juries. They also issued punishments as they saw fit.

When did vigilantes start in the American West?
The first vigilance committee was set up in 1851.

Where did vigilantes start in the American West?
The first vigilance committee was set up in San Francisco *(p.37)*.

Who set up the first of the vigilance committees in the American West?
Businessmen in San Francisco *(p.37)*, who felt the legal system was too corrupt to trust, set up their own system. The first vigilance committee consisted of around 200 men.

What did the vigilantes do in 1851 in the American West?
In 1851, the vigilance committee dealt with 89 suspects:
- ☑ Half the suspects tried by the vigilance committee were found not guilty.
- ☑ A quarter of the suspects were deported.
- ☑ 15 were handed over to federal law enforcement officers.
- ☑ The remaining suspects were hanged.

How did vigilantes in the American West come to an end?
Once citizens felt law and order *(p.38)* had been reestablished, they closed the committee in San Francisco *(p.37)*. However, the idea spread to other areas.

How effective were the vigilantes in the American West?
Vigilance committees were often very effective as they could act more quickly than actual law officers. They created fear, preventing more crimes.

What was the problem with vigilantes in the American West?
The major issue with vigilantes was that they could be unfair and unjust. They acted according to their own rules, whims, alliances and decisions. Often guilt was decided before a person was captured, and sometimes people were lynched as a result. Vigilante behaviour could be worse than that of those they persecuted.

> **DID YOU KNOW?**
>
> **Some vigilante groups were highly respected.**
> In San Francisco they took over the Democrat Party, and some members became politicians.

THE CAUSES OF THE AMERICAN CIVIL WAR
A war between the northern and southern states, which had a devastating impact and changed the course of American history.

What was the American Civil War?
The American Civil War was an internal conflict between the northern and southern states of the USA.

When did the American Civil War happen?
The American Civil War was fought from 1861 to 1865.

Why was the American Civil War fought?
There were 5 main causes of the American Civil War.
- ☑ The debate around slavery meant that slave owners in the south disagreed with abolitionists in the north. The South wanted to keep slavery, because it provided plantation owners with a free workforce.
- ☑ The nature of the US Government meant there was tension between states and the federal government about who had the right to make laws. The arguments often centered around slavery.
- ☑ Westward expansion meant that the issue of slavery was always discussed. New states were admitted to the Union, and it needed to be established whether they would be 'free' states or 'slave' states.
- ☑ States that felt their liberty to make laws was being threatened said they would secede if they felt their views were not properly represented in Congress.
- ☑ There were economic differences. The climate in the South favoured agriculture, particularly cotton and tobacco growing. It was very profitable and relied on slave labour. However, the North was industrialised, and wasn't prepared to compete with slave labour.

What were the economic effects of the American Civil War?
There were 7 main economic effects of the American Civil War.
- ☑ The only real area of growth in both North and South was munitions production.
- ☑ The economy in the North was short of raw materials, as trade with the South was virtually eliminated.
- ☑ The economy in the South was inferior to that in the North, which had already industrialised. As a result the South was hit hardest, and couldn't adequately supply its army.
- ☑ Farms across the South were ruined by war, and crops and animals were confiscated. There were food riots later in the war, due to shortages.

- ☑ Cotton production in the South decreased dramatically. It also lost access to its European cotton markets, due to a naval blockade by the Union.
- ☑ Since the South had no real currency of its own, it suffered huge rates of inflation. Inflation was over 9,000% per year at its peak.
- ☑ The railroad system was severely damaged.

What were the social effects of the American Civil War?
There were several social effects of the American Civil War.
- ☑ Family life was disrupted for many Americans, who experienced conscription into the war effort.
- ☑ Since the North blockaded the South, people in the South suffered huge shortages of many things, including food and clothing.
- ☑ Many southerners found that their homes and properties had become part of a battleground, which created a large number of refugees.
- ☑ Some southern towns were placed under the control of the army (martial law), so people's rights were restricted.
- ☑ Since guerrilla warfare was common in the South, many southerners found they were living close to extreme and frightening violence.
- ☑ The war resulted in 600,000 dead and 400,000 wounded.

How did the American Civil War end?
The American Civil War ended in April 1865, when Robert E. Lee surrendered at Appomattox Courthouse in Virginia.

DID YOU KNOW?

The Union army was multicultural.
- ✓ The Union army (of the North) had soldiers from across Europe.
- ✓ In 1863 the Union army allowed black soldiers to serve; but they were not paid the same wage as their white colleagues.

THE HOMESTEAD ACT
An opportunity for white settlers to have a better chance at life.

What was the Homestead Act?
The Homestead Act was a law, signed by Lincoln, which gave farmers 160 acres of Plains land (called a homestead). The land was free so long as it was successfully farmed for five years. It cost just $10 to register and claim this land.

When did the Homestead Act become law?
The Homestead Act was signed into law in 1862.

How was land distributed before the Homestead Act?
Before the Homestead Act the government owned all the land in the West, then sold land at $1 an acre. This was too expensive for most people to afford.

Who could claim land using the Homestead Act?
To file a claim you needed to be over 21 years old (unless you were an ex-soldier), and either single or the head of a family. This opened up claiming to more people: those in the process of becoming a US citizen, ex-slaves, and women. Native Americans *(p.17)* were still excluded.

What were the rules to the Homestead Act?
To prevent business owners snapping up land and making a profit from it there were strict rules. A person could not file numerous claims. They had to live on the land, build a house, plant at least five acres of crops, and work it for five years.

What was 'proving up' under the Homestead Act?
If the rules were followed for 5 years the homestead could be bought out fully for $30. This was called 'proving up'.

What did the Homestead Act achieve?
As a result of the Homestead Act, over 6 million acres of government land and over 80 million acres of public land were settled. Nebraska's population grew so much that it became a state in 1867.

How did the Homestead Act help migration?
The Homestead Act encouraged people to migrate to the West, who would not have been able to do so before. Nebraska alone was boosted by 123,000 immigrants - almost half the population of the state.

What were the problems with the Homestead Act?
There were 5 main limitations to the Homestead Act.
- Proving up was not common, so much of the land stayed as homesteads. By 1900 only 24 million acres had been proved up; and, overall, 60% of the land was never proved up.
- Although a lot of land was given over to homesteads, more land went to the railroads (300 million acres), and to cattle ranchers, who paid highly for it.
- Many homesteaders bought their land from the railroad companies, instead of through the government scheme.
- Rich landowners sometimes abused the scheme by getting employees to claim land as a homesteader *(p.46)*, then handing the rights over to the landowner.
- Part of the scheme allowed people to pay $1.25 an acre for land, which they were allowed to sell after six months of living there and ploughing at least an acre of it. They could earn profits using the scheme.

DID YOU KNOW?

There were certain requirements to get free land.
In order to get the land, you had to be over 21 or the head of a household.

THE TRANSCONTINENTAL RAILROAD
Impressive railroads which connected east to west.

What were transcontinental railroads?
Transcontinental railroads were the railways which linked eastern USA to the western states.

When were the transcontinental railroads built?
The first transcontinental railroad, the Union-Pacific, was built between 1863 and 1869. Another four were constructed by 1900.

Where did the transcontinental railroads start and end?
The first transcontinental railroad ran between Omaha, Nebraska, and Sacramento in California.

What were the problems with the transcontinental railroad?
There were 5 main problems with the construction of the transcontinental railroad.
- The railroad was costly, and it was difficult to raise money for its construction.
- The railroad had to navigate difficult terrain, including mountains and deserts.
- Hostile Native Americans *(p. 17)* attacked railroad workers.
- It was difficult to find enough people willing to work on the railroads.
- The living and working conditions were terrible.

Why were transcontinental railroads so important?
Transcontinental railroads were important because they helped people move onto the Great Plains and travel across the United States. Railroad companies offered cheap land next to the tracks, which helped more people settle on the plains.

What impact did the transcontinental railroad have on settlers and farmers?
The railroad had several effects on settlers and farmers:
- Travel became significantly cheaper and more convenient.
- Towns and businesses grew rapidly around the railroad as it brought in more people.
- Transporting goods became easier and cheaper. This meant farmers could make more money by selling their grain further away.
- More products were brought to settlers: machinery, household items and luxuries became more widely available.
- Many immigrants from Europe were able to settle with great success.

What impact did the transcontinental railroad have on Native Americans?
The railroad had several effects on Native Americans *(p. 17)*.
- The railroad routes and tracks encroached even more on their lands, forcing them to move away.
- To try and prevent railroads being built they attacked railroad surveyors. This led to conflict with the US Army.
- The railroad caused a further reduction in buffalo *(p. 20)* numbers as it reduced the grassland they needed for food. It also brought in hunters, who killed great numbers of buffalo.
- Some tribes, including the Pawnee, Omaha and Winnebago, signed treaties with the US government and moved onto reservations.

What impact did the transcontinental railroad have on the USA?
The railroad had a significant impact on the USA as a whole.
- The railroad boosted the economy. As it connected east and west, trade became easier and quicker. It also opened Asia up to American markets.
- Many Americans felt Manifest Destiny had been achieved, and America was now becoming a united nation.

What impact did the transcontinental railroad have on the cattle industry?
The railroad had an impact on the cattle industry *(p. 53)*, as it enabled cattle to be transported vast distances relatively quickly and cheaply. This meant cattle ranchers could sell their cattle in the eastern markets where prices were higher, making larger profits.

What impact did the transcontinental railroad have on the homesteaders?
The railroad had 3 main effects on homesteaders.
- Transport was faster and easier, making it simpler to visit friends and family.
- Homesteaders could bring in goods to make their lives easier. They could order goods from the east using mail order, such as from the Sears, Roebuck & Company catalogue.
- Towns grew rapidly around the railroad, which allowed communities to form. Homesteaders could discuss farming ideas, socialise, and sell and buy products.

> **DID YOU KNOW?**
> The Union-Pacific railroad was 1,776 miles long.

THE PACIFIC RAILROAD ACT
A scheme to connect the newly established lands of the west coast.

What was the Pacific Railroad Act?
The Pacific Railroad Act was a government scheme to encourage the building of transcontinental railroads to the west of America.

When was the Pacific Railroad Act introduced?
The Pacific Railroad Act was passed in 1862.

Why was the Pacific Railroad Act introduced?
The railroads in the USA were extensive. but only went as far west as the Missouri River. It was believed that if transcontinental railroads could be built, migration to the west would be easier and towns would develop more quickly.

Who did the Pacific Railroad Act assign to build the railroad?
Two companies were set up to build the railroad, starting at different ends. Union Pacific started in Omaha and built west, while Central Pacific started in Sacramento and built east.

How did the Pacific Railroad Act ensure the railroad was completed?
The Pacific Railroad Act was designed to encourage companies to take on a risky project where profits might be non-existent.
- The Act removed Native American *(p.17)* rights to land on any part of the route.
- The government loaned each company $16,000 for every mile of railroad it laid. This increased to $48,000 for mountainous parts of the route. Over $61 million was loaned in total.
- The Act allocated 45 million acres of public land to the companies, for them to sell or otherwise do with as they wished.

> **DID YOU KNOW?**
>
> **The building of the railroad was a multicultural effort.**
> - ✓ In the west, much of the railroad was built by Chinese labourers.
> - ✓ In the east the majority of workers were Irish labourers, as well ex-Confederates from the Civil War, European immigrants, and freed slaves.

RAILROAD COMPANIES
Two railroad companies competed, risking the lives of their workers to turn a profit.

Who were the railroad companies?
The Union Pacific and Central Pacific railroad companies built the transcontinental railroad *(p.42)* from 1862, under the Pacific Railroad Act.

What problems did the railroad companies have while building?
The railroad companies almost went bankrupt building the transcontinental railroad *(p.42)*. This was because it was a huge and costly feat of engineering.

How did the railroad companies pay their investors?
It was discovered Union Pacific was overcharging the government for its work on the railroad so the company could pay its investors more money.

How did the railroad companies encourage immigration?
The railroad companies encouraged immigration to the western states.
- ✓ The Union Pacific and Central Pacific railroad companies both had a Bureau of Immigration to persuade people from other countries to come to the western states.
- ✓ The bureau offered tours, loans, and lots of incentives to migrate.

How successful were the railroad companies?
The railroad companies were very successful in attracting migrants.
- ✓ The railroad companies settled more people in the west than the government did under the Homestead Act *(p.41)*, allocating 200 million acres by 1880.
- ✓ 10,000 Scandinavians moved to Nebraska due to the activities of one bureau agent. Another agent, C B Schmidt, encouraged 60,000 Germans to go to Kansas.

> **DID YOU KNOW?**
>
> It is estimated around 12,000 men lost their lives in the building of the railroads.

HOMESTEADERS
Land was available to settlers, who had enough savings, to maintain the land.

What was a homesteader?
A homesteader was a farmer who accepted land under the Homestead Act *(p.41)*.

Why did homesteaders move west?
There were 3 main reasons why there was a rise in the number of people moving west after the Civil War.
- The US Government introduced new laws to encourage settlement of the west.
- The construction of transcontinental railroads made it easier to travel west and to transport supplies there.
- Many ex-soldiers and ex-slaves wanted to start a new life after the Civil War.

What problems did the homesteaders experience?
Homesteaders had a number of challenges when trying to farm the Plains.
- There was a lack of materials for building homes and fences.
- There was a lack of fuel for fires and cooking.
- There was a lack of water from rivers and rainfall.
- The weather could be unpredictable and dangerous.
- The soil was tough, and difficult to plough *(p.48)*.
- There was a problem with pests. Crops could be trampled by buffalo *(p.20)*, or eaten by swarms of grasshoppers.
- Many of the crops that homesteaders farmed, such as maize, did not grow well on the Plains.
- Homesteads were spread out, so there was a lack of a close community for social interaction, goods and services.

How did the homesteaders solve their problems?
While many homesteaders' attempts to farm failed, some did discover solutions to the problems. A number of new ideas and inventions helped make life easier for the homesteaders.
- Sod, or tough mud, was dug up and used to build houses.
- Barbed wire *(p.48)* was invented by Joseph Glidden in 1874, which made it possible for homesteaders to fence their land.
- Homesteaders used buffalo *(p.20)* chips (dried buffalo dung) as fuel.
- In 1854, Daniel Halladay *(p.47)* invented a windmill *(p.47)* that helped to pump underground water to the surface.
- Farmers used 'dry farming *(p.69)*' methods to keep moisture in the soil.
- In 1830, John Deere made the 'sodbuster' plough *(p.48)*, which could cope with the tough earth on the Plains.
- New machinery, such as threshers and reapers, were developed. Large areas of land were particularly suited to mechanisation.
- Russian settlers on the Plains brought new, hardy varieties of crop, such as Turkey Red wheat.
- As the railroads developed, supplies were brought to the homesteaders on the Plains. It also meant they could travel more easily.

DID YOU KNOW?
Land was purchased then resold to European immigrants.
Promises of a better life were publicised in newspapers in England, the Netherlands and Germany.

DANIEL HALLADAY

An inventor, engineer and businessman.

Who was Daniel Halladay?

Daniel Halladay invented a windmill *(p.47)* in 1854. It was also known as a water pump, as it was designed to bring water to the surface. It changed direction with the wind.

> **DID YOU KNOW?**
>
> Daniel Halladay had a long life, living to the age of 89.

WINDMILL

An incredible invention that helped farmers by supplying water to new lands.

How did windmills help homesteaders?

Windmills were used to bring water to the surface, where it could then be used to irrigate crops. A windmill could pump water from a depth of up to 30 feet.

When did homesteaders begin using windmills?

A 'self-governing' windmill was invented in 1854. Steel blades were added in 1870.

Who invented the windmill used by homesteaders?

Daniel Halladay *(p.47)* invented the windmill, or wind-pump, which brought water to the surface.

What problems were there with the windmill used by the homesteaders?

If the water was more than 30 feet below the surface, it could not be pumped. Until the steel blades were added, the windmills needed frequent oiling and often broke.

How had windmills developed by the 1880s?

By the 1880s, many problems with the windmills/wind-pumps had been solved. They were made completely of metal and only needed oiling once a year. They were stronger and able to pump more water from deeper in the ground.

> **DID YOU KNOW?**
>
> **Windmills quickly became a key component of the west's landscape.**
>
> Most painted landscapes pictures of the American West would feature a windmill.

BARBED WIRE
A way to protect animals and crops from the indigenous animals of the west.

How was barbed wire used by homesteaders?
Barbed wire was used to protect crops from being eaten by livestock.

When was barbed wire introduced?
Barbed wire was first used in the west in 1874.

What were the advantages of barbed wire to homesteaders?
Timber was difficult and expensive to transport. Barbed wire was a cheaper and easier way to fence off and protect crops.

What problems did homesteaders have with barbed wire?
Early types of barbed wire were poor quality, breaking easily and susceptible to rust. In time, barbed wire became more expensive.

DID YOU KNOW?

Joseph Glidden was known as the 'father of barbed wire'.
His invention made him a millionaire.

SULKY PLOW
An invention to get rid of unwanted crops.

What was a sulky plow?
The sulky plow was a ride-on steel plough that could successfully work the weeds, grass and sod of the Great Plains.

How many sulky plows were sold?
50,000 were sold in the first six years after its invention.

What were the problems with the sulky plow?
Sulky plows were expensive. Push ploughs were cheaper, and six of these were bought for every one sulky plow.

DID YOU KNOW?

The sulky plow was nicknamed the 'sod-buster'.

MENNONITES
A religious group that came to America to farm.

Who were the Mennonites?
The Mennonites were farmers from the grasslands of Russia. A group of them was persuaded by railroad agents to move to the Great Plains.

What did the Mennonites grow in the Great Plains?
Mennonites were used to farming Turkey Red wheat, and they found this grew well in Kansas.

> **DID YOU KNOW?**
>
> The Mennonites were part of the Anabaptist sect of Protestantism which originally developed in the Netherlands.

RED TURKEY
A type of wheat found to grow well on the Great Plains.

What was Red Turkey?
Red Turkey is a type of wheat. Homesteaders found it hard to find crops that grew well on the Great Plains, but Red Turkey provided a breakthrough.

THE TIMBER AND CULTURE ACT
More land given to homesteaders in order to plant trees.

What was the Timber Culture Act?
The Timber Culture Act was a law which gave homesteaders 160 acres of land in addition to that permitted by the Homestead Act *(p.41)*, so long as they planted 40 acres of it with trees.

When was the Timber Culture Act signed?
The Timber Culture Act was signed in 1873.

Why was the Timber Culture Act important?
Trees were extremely important in the West. They could be used as a barrier to the strong winds; houses could be built from it; and it could be burnt as a fuel. However, there were few trees on the Great Plains, so timber was rare, and expensive to bring to the Plains. The Timber Culture Act was designed to encourage the planting of trees.

What were the problems with the Timber Culture Act?
Many trees died, as they did not have enough water. Also, people used the Act to claim more land, which they sold for a profit after a few years.

What were the successes of the Timber Culture Act?
In Minnesota large numbers of trees were planted successfully.

> ### DID YOU KNOW?
> **Trees were important to life in the west.**
> They provided fuel, and could be used to build houses.

HELL ON WHEELS
Lawless towns adjacent to the newly built railways.

 What was Hell on Wheels?
Hell on Wheels was the name given to new towns that grew up around the transcontinental railroad *(p.42)*. They were considered the most lawless of places, especially when the cowboys celebrated the end of a working week.

COW TOWNS
Troublesome towns centred on farming areas and the transport and sale of cattle.

 What was a cow town?
Cow towns (or cattle towns) were towns that grew up around the transcontinental railroad *(p.42)*. They were a hub for transporting cattle on the railway to the markets of the east.

 Why were the cow towns considered lawless?
Cowboys were paid their wages after loading the cattle onto the trains. They then celebrated, and this could lead to trouble.

> ### DID YOU KNOW?
> **After a long period of herding cattle, cowboys often went on massive spending sprees.**
> They spent their money in brothels, saloons and gambling halls.

ABILENE

The first cow town was in Kansas.

What was Abilene?
Abilene in Kansas was an example of a cow-town *(p.50)*. Thanks to John McCoy *(p.54)* it was the first cow-town.

How did the population of Abilene change due to the railroad?
The population of Abilene grew from 500 to 7,000 people.

How lawless was Abilene?
Abilene, and other cow towns, were lawless in a number of ways.
- Cowboys used the saloons and bars to drink and gamble. Cheating and swindling at the card table were not uncommon.
- Cowboys were paid their wages after loading the cattle onto the trains. They then celebrated and this could lead to lawless trouble.
- Gunfights and murder were frequent and attempts to stop them were futile. A sign saying guns were banned in Abilene was shot so badly that nobody could read it.
- A jail was built in Abilene in 1870, but it was demolished by cowboys.
- In early 1870, Thomas Smith *(p.51)* was appointed town marshal of Abilene. He was killed in November the same year. Wild Bill Hickok *(p.52)* was appointed marshall in 1871, but he lasted in the job for just a few months.

When did the Kansas Pacific Railroad reach Abilene?
The Kansas Pacific Railroad reached Abilene in 1867.

Why did Abilene become the first cow town?
Abilene became the first cow-town *(p.50)* when Joseph McCoy *(p.54)* built cattle ports alongside the railroad there.

> **DID YOU KNOW?**
>
> **Crowds of cowboys would sometimes rampage through the towns, wrecking everything in their path.**
> They even destroyed a newly constructed jail!

THOMAS SMITH

A town marshall who tried to stop the lawlessness.

Who was Thomas Smith?
Thomas Smith was the town marshall appointed to Abilene *(p.51)* in early 1870.

What did Thomas Smith do in Abilene?
He introduced a ban on carrying guns and used his boxing skills to enforce the rules!

How did Thomas Smith die?

Thomas Smith was shot and then decapitated with an axe in November 1870.

DID YOU KNOW?

He was paid a commission for every criminal who was convicted.

On top of his salary of $150 per month, he received $2 for each person convicted of a crime.

WILD BILL HICKOK

A town marshall who returned Abilene to its lawless ways.

 Who was Wild Bill Hickok?

Wild Bill Hickok was appointed as Abilene's *(p.51)* town marshall in 1871 and sacked within a year for a number of misdeeds. As well as being involved in a number of suspicious shootings, he was accused of spending his time gambling, rather than enforcing the law.

THE RENO GANG

A gang of established criminals who brought terror to the communities in its path.

 Who were the Reno Gang?

The Reno Gang was a group of deserters from the Civil War. They were conmen, thieves and train robbers, and often got away with crimes by bribing law officials.

 What crimes did the Reno Gang commit?

The Reno Gang committed train robberies. Their first, in 1866, saw the gang break open a safe and steal $16,000. They carried out more robberies in 1867 and 1868. In their fourth robbery they got away with $96,000.

 What happened to the Reno Gang?

John Reno was caught in 1866. Another gang member was captured during the fifth robbery and gave up the rest of the gang in return for a reduced sentence. After their arrest, they were lynched by a mob of vigilantes.

DID YOU KNOW?

The gang was eventually captured by Pinkerton detectives.

- ✓ The Pinkerton National Detective Agency was used as a private law enforcement agency.
- ✓ The agency's founder, Allan J Pinkerton, became famous when he claimed to have foiled an assassination plot against Abraham Lincoln.

THE TEXAN CATTLE INDUSTRY
An expansion of the cattle industry which created a profitable market for beef.

What was the Texan cattle industry?
When Texas gained its independence from Mexico in 1836, it also took over the Mexican cattle industry.

Who worked for the Texan cattle industry?
Men rode for the industry herding cattle from one place to another. They were called 'cowboys'.

Where did the Texan cattle industry move the cattle to and from?
Cattle were moved from the south to New Orleans. They were also taken through Missouri to Sedalia and St Louis, where they could then be transported to markets in the north of America.

What problems did the Texan cattle industry have?
The cattle from Texas carried a disease called 'Texas fever *(p.53)*', which was infectious and transmitted by the cattle tick. As a consequence, farmers in Missouri and South Kansas formed vigilance *(p.39)* committees to block the routes until quarantine laws were put in place.

What happened to the Texan cattle industry after the American Civil War?
The American Civil War *(p.40)* had 4 major consequences for the cattle industry:
- Consumer demand for beef in the north of America grew.
- Advancements in the meat-packing industry meant it was easier to turn the cattle into meat.
- Many cattle herds had not been managed during the war, so there were now 5 million cows in Texas, mostly of the Longhorn breed.
- A cow in the north became worth $40, as opposed to $5 in the south. Cowboys from Texas tried to organise a huge cattle drive to the north in order to get the better price. They were prevented by farmers in Kansas, who were worried about Texas fever *(p.53)* outbreaks.

What impact did the Texan cattle industry have on the buffalo?
As cattle numbers grew, the buffalo *(p.20)* herds declined. These animals were both grazing livestock, so were competing for the same food. This had an impact on the Native American *(p.17)* tribes, whose way of life relied on the buffalo.

> **DID YOU KNOW?**
> In 1865 it was estimated there were 5 million cows in Texas.

TEXAS FEVER
A disease that was deadly to cows and could result in great losses.

What was 'Texas fever'?
Texas fever was a cattle disease that often resulted in the animals dying. It is no longer prevalent in the USA as the tick that caused it has been eliminated.

Why was Texas fever a problem?
Texas cattle were driven on routes across Missouri and Kansas, which could result in the disease spreading.

What happened as a result of Texas cattle fever?
Quarantine laws were passed to prevent infected cattle from entering Missouri in 1855, and then Kansas in 1859.

DID YOU KNOW?

Symptoms included bloody urine, a high fever, anaemia, and eventually death.

THE QUARANTINE LAWS FOR CATTLE
A law put in place to stop the spread of Texas fever.

What quarantine cattle laws were passed?
After outbreaks of Texas fever *(p.53)*, quarantine laws were passed to prevent infected cattle from entering other states. Missouri passed their laws in 1855, and Kansas followed suit in 1859.

JOSEPH MCCOY
A livestock trader from Chicago who transformed Abilene.

Who was Joseph McCoy?
Joseph McCoy turned Abilene *(p.51)* into a new transit port for cattle drives, which made him very rich.

How did Joseph McCoy make Abilene a new transit port?
McCoy purchased land and built huge stockyards in which to hold cattle. He negotiated with the Kansas Pacific Railroad and built a depot right next to the railroad track, where cattle could be loaded onto trains. He also built a hotel to house the cowboys and clearly mapped out the Chisholm Trail *(p.55)* they used for the cattle drives.

How did Joseph McCoy get people to use his facilities?
McCoy advertised the facilities he had created and sent guides to bring cowboys safely along the trail.

How successful was Joseph McCoy?
McCoy became very wealthy. He managed to get 35,000 cattle driven along the Chisholm Trail *(p.55)* by the end of 1867. Another 3 million had followed by 1872. His success led to Abilene *(p.51)* being the first 'cow-town *(p.50)*'.

DID YOU KNOW?

McCoy ran for US Congress as a Democrat. He was unsuccessful.

THE CHISHOLM TRAIL
A trail that took cattle from Texas to Kansas.

What was the Chisholm Trail?
The Chisholm Trail was the route from Kansas to Texas which became popular among cowboys in the 1860s, thanks to Joseph McCoy *(p.54)*.

How long did the Chisholm Trail take to ride?
The journey along the Chisholm Trail could take between 2 and 3 months.

> **DID YOU KNOW?**
> Around 2,500 cattle and between 10 and 12 horses would travel along the trail on each drive.

THE GOODNIGHT-LOVING TRAIL
A trail that took cattle from Texas to Wyoming.

What was the Goodnight-Loving Trail?
The Goodnight-Loving Trail ran from Texas to Wyoming, through hostile Comanche Indian territory. The cattle industry *(p.53)* led to the growth of Wyoming.

When was the Goodnight-Loving Trail established?
It was established in 1866.

Who established the Goodnight-Loving Trail?
Charles Goodnight *(p.56)* and Oliver Loving *(p.56)* established the Goodnight-Loving Trail.

How long did the Goodnight-Loving Trail take?
The journey along the Goodnight-Loving Trail took about 6 months.

When was the Goodnight-Loving Trail used?
Goodnight and Loving used the trail a few times, either together or alone.
- In 1866, with 18 cowboys, they drove 2,000 cattle along the trail.
- 1,200 of those cattle were then driven further along the trail, and sold to John Iliff *(p.57)*.
- In 1868 they drove cattle to Cheyenne, Wyoming.
- Other cattle drivers started to use the trail and Wyoming flourished.

> **DID YOU KNOW?**
> The first trail consisted of 2,000 Texas Longhorn cattle and 18 cow-hands.

CHARLES GOODNIGHT

Charles Loving was a cattle rancher known as 'the father of the Texas Panhandle'.

Who was Charles Goodnight?
Charles Goodnight was a cattle rancher who established the Goodnight-loving Trail with Oliver Loving *(p. 56)*.

What did Charles Goodnight do?
Goodnight drove cattle from Texas to Wyoming, as they could get four times the amount of money when they sold them there. He continued after Loving's death, and drove cattle to Colorado too.

How successful was Charles Goodnight?
Goodnight was so successful that, by 1876, he was able to grow his ranch *(p. 59)* to over 1 million acres.

> **DID YOU KNOW?**
>
> **He was also interested in herding bison.**
> The legacy of his bison farming has survived and his herd still exists today.

OLIVER LOVING

Goodnight's partner in the Goodnight-Loving Trail.

Who was Oliver Loving?
Oliver Loving was a cattle rancher who established the Goodnight-loving Trail with Charles Goodnight *(p. 56)*.

How did Oliver Loving die?
Loving died in 1867 after being injured during an attack by Comanche Indians.

> **DID YOU KNOW?**
>
> **Not only were they business partners, but they were also close friends.**
> - ✓ Goodnight was at Loving's bedside for the two weeks it took Loving to die from his injuries.
> - ✓ He even carried a picture of Loving in his wallet.

JOHN ILIFF
A millionaire who profited greatly from a cheap herd of cattle.

Who was John Iliff?
John Iliff was the first millionaire in Denver, Colorado. He bought a herd of cattle in 1861, getting them cheaply as they were exhausted from the long drive from the south. He grazed them on the Plains, then sold them for beef at a huge profit.

Where was John Iliff's ranch?
Iliff's ranch *(p.59)* was between Denver, Colorado and Cheyenne in Wyoming. By 1870 he had in excess of 26,000 cattle on more than 16,000 acres of land.

Who did John Iliff sell beef to?
Iliff sold beef to mining towns, reservations, the government, and to the people building the railroad.

Why was John Iliff so successful?
Iliff succeeded because he saw a gap in the local regional market. Instead of cattle being brought to the north on trails, he changed the industry by raising them on the Plains.

> **DID YOU KNOW?**
>
> **Iliff was nicknamed 'the Cattle King of the Plains.'**
> He was given this nickname because of his huge success in selling his cattle, near and far.

CATTLE TRAILS
The route that took cattle from ranch to market.

What is a cattle trail?
Cattle trails were the routes used by cowboys to drive cattle from ranch *(p.59)* to market. They needed to be planned out, to ensure there was enough grass and water along the way to feed the cattle.

What were the main cattle trails?
From 1866 to the 1880s, several trails were established:

- ☑ The Shawnee Trail. This was used until 1866, when outbreaks of Texas fever *(p.53)* caused farmers to block it. It ran from San Antonio in Texas to Kansas City or Sedalia.
- ☑ The Goodnight-loving Trail, used from 1866 to the 1880s. It was established from Texas to Cheyenne, through New Mexico and California.
- ☑ The Chisholm Trail *(p.55)*, used from 1867 to 1872. It started in San Antonio, Texas, and finished in Wichita, Ellsworth, or Abilene *(p.51)*.
- ☑ The Western Trail. This was used from 1876 to 1884, after the establishment of Dodge City in Kansas. It went from San Antonio, Texas, to Ogallala in Nebraska.

How were Native Americans affected by the cattle trails?

Native Americans *(p.17)* felt those using the cattle trails were trespassers. They patrolled and monitored the trails, stole horses and cattle, and even attacked cowboys when they passed by. This led to conflicts with the US Army.

> **DID YOU KNOW?**
>
> The average journey on the cattle trail lasted 3 to 5 months!

CATTLE BARONS

Influential ranchers who had big stakes in the cattle industry and beyond.

 What was a cattle baron?

The term 'cattle baron' refers to the rich men who ran the cattle ranch *(p.59)* industry from the 1870s, in areas such as Colorado and Wyoming. They were also influential in local politics and business, and owned much of the land.

COWBOYS

An exciting career for young men in the Wild West.

 What is a cowboy?

Cowboys were the men who drove the cattle along the cattle trails, from the ranches in the south to markets in the north.

 What was life like for the cowboys?

A cowboy's life involved moving around 3,000 cattle at a time along the trails. They typically worked in teams of 12, with a trail boss to manage the process. They carried all their supplies and built a camp each night, sleeping in the open and taking turns to keep watch. They got paid at the end of each trail and spent their money on new clothes, alcohol, gambling and prostitutes.

 What were the problems with a cowboy's life?

Cowboys had to overcome a number of problems and hardships:

- ☑ Cattle are dangerous. A stampede could cause injury or death.
- ☑ Riding at night. Stampedes often happened after dark, which meant cowboys had to trust their horses to be sure-footed.
- ☑ Dangerous animals. Wild animals posed a risk, as the cowboys lived for months at a time in the open air on the cattle trails.
- ☑ Native Americans *(p.17)*. Cowboys often needed to cross Native American lands, so had to negotiate with them to avoid conflict. Sometimes negotiation failed and they had to fight.
- ☑ Attacks by outlaws.

How much were the cowboys paid?
A cowboy could earn $25-30 a month on the Chisholm Trail *(p.55)*. A trail boss could earn $100 a month.

Did the cowboys follow laws?
Once paid, cowboys would often cause problems in towns. They often broke laws to do with alcohol, prostitution and gambling.

What was being a cowboy like on a ranch?
Cowboys on ranches still looked after cattle, but they did not travel along the trails. Fewer cowboys were needed to keep an eye on cattle that roamed the vast ranches. In spring, they rounded up the animals, separated them into groups, and branded them according to ownership. Cowboys lived in communal bunkhouses on the ranches.

What did the cowboys do in the winter months?
Cowboys could not work the trails in winter and there was also less work on the ranches. Instead, cowboys often got jobs in the towns or did odd jobs around ranches.

How old were cowboys?
Being a cowboy was a young man's life, and most were in their 20s. When they were older they could find maintenance work or start their own ranches and employ others.

Why did Native Americans join cowboys?
As the cattle industry *(p.53)* grew, the number of buffalo *(p.20)* declined severely. With the loss of their livelihoods, many Native Americans *(p.17)* became cowboys.

> **DID YOU KNOW?**
> Cowboys would often go weeks without washing their clothes!

CATTLE RANCHES
A place for large numbers of cattle.

What was a cattle ranch?
A cattle ranch was a large area of farmland where cattle were kept.

Who started the first ranch?
John Iliff *(p.57)* started the first cattle ranch in 1861.

What happened on the ranch in the winter?
In winter the cattle were allowed to roam free, so there was little work for the cowboys. The few that remained on the ranch used their time to fix equipment, check on animals that got into trouble in harsh weather, and make plans for spring.

What happened on the ranch in the spring?
In the spring the cattle needed to be rounded up, branded with their owner's mark, and driven closer to the ranch.

How did the ranches use the railroad?
The ranches took their cattle to the railroad for transportation, instead of driving them along trails to market. It took days rather than months, and was much less costly and dangerous.

How big were ranches?
Typically, ranches were over 2,000 acres, although many were a lot bigger. They also used public land for grazing.

Why was there rivalry between the ranches and the homesteaders?
There were 7 important reasons for the rivalry between the cattle ranchers and the homesteaders:
- ☑ Homesteaders could claim public land under the Homestead Act *(p.41)*. This land was already being used as additional grazing land by the cattle ranchers.
- ☑ Ranchers sometimes claimed land under the Homestead Act *(p.41)*, which contained the water source for the surrounding land. This put the homesteaders off making a claim there.
- ☑ As they bought up different areas of land, the ranchers could make some public land impossible for homesteaders to access.
- ☑ Workers on cattle ranches put in claims for land and then handed the rights to the owner of the ranch.
- ☑ Violence was used by some ranchers to threaten homesteaders away from claiming public land.
- ☑ Some ranchers accused homesteaders of crimes such as 'stealing a cow', which carried a severe punishment.
- ☑ Ranchers sometimes took homesteaders to court over land. Because the homesteaders could not afford lawyers and court costs, they often gave in to the ranchers' bullying.

Why was there rivalry between the ranches and sheep farmers?
Ranchers and sheep farmers both used public land for grazing, which brought them into conflict. The cattle ranchers put up fences which were cut down by the sheep farmers. This led to violence and court cases. The cattle ranchers were involved in politics and had the right connections, and sheep farmers often lost in the courts.

Why did Native Americans join ranches?
Many Native Americans *(p.17)* sought work on the ranches after losing their livelihoods - the growth of the cattle industry *(p.53)* meant the number of buffalo *(p.20)* was severely reduced.

DID YOU KNOW?

Life on the ranch was difficult.

Not only was the work hard but there wasn't much to do at the end of the day. Some ranches even banned their workers from gambling.

THE PEACE POLICY
An attempt to create peaceful relations with the Native Americans.

What was the 'Peace Policy'?
The Peace Policy was meant to calm tensions between the white Americans and Native Americans *(p.17)* by improving management of the reservations.

When was the Peace Policy?
The Peace Policy was implemented in 1868.

Who proposed the Peace Policy?
The Peace Policy was proposed by President Ulysses S Grant.

What were the main points in the Peace Policy?
The Peace Policy had a number of aims:

- It aimed to remove the corrupt men who currently managed the reservations and replace them with Quakers. It was believed these religious men would be fair, just and peaceful, due to their beliefs.
- $2 million was put aside to aid and care for the Native Americans *(p.17)* on reservations. It was also used to gather up any tribes not yet on a reservation *(p.24)* and settle them there.

> **DID YOU KNOW?**
> The 'S' in Ulysses S Grant does not stand for anything.

ELY S PARKER
US Congress declared that 'Indians should be treated as wards of the state.'

Who was Ely S Parker?
Ely S Parker was appointed the Commissioner of Indian Affairs in 1868.

What did Ely S. Parker believe?
Parker believed the Native Americans *(p.17)* could not be negotiated with, and should be treated as 'helpless and ignorant wards'. This meant they were considered unable to make their own decisions, so must obey the government's orders. This led to the Indian Appropriation Act of 1871.

> **DID YOU KNOW?**
> **Ely S Parker was Native American.**
> He was seen as a traitor by his own people, as he gained prominence in Washington and white society.

THE 1871 INDIAN APPROPRIATIONS ACT
An extension of the first Indian Appropriations Act.

What was the Second Indian Appropriations Act?

The second Indian Appropriations Act took power away from individual tribes, and brought all Native Americans *(p.17)* under US law as 'wards' of the US government.

When was the Second Indian Appropriations Act signed?

The second Indian Appropriations Act was signed in 1871.

LITTLE CROW
The fierce chief of the Dakota Sioux tribe.

Who was Little Crow

Little Crow was the chief of a band within the Dakota Sioux *(p.62)* tribe of Native Americans *(p.17)*. He and his tribe lived in Minnesota.

How did Little Crow die?

Little Crow was shot by a hunter, who scalped him so he could claim the bounty on him. Later, another man cut off his head.

> **DID YOU KNOW?**
>
> **He tried to adapt to customs of the United States**
> When visiting President Buchanan he wore European clothing. He even joined the Episcopal Church and became a farmer.

THE DAKOTA SIOUX
'One does not sell the land people walk on.'
- a saying attributed to Crazy Horse

Who were the Dakota Sioux?

The Dakota Sioux were Native Americans *(p.17)* who lived in the Minnesota area.

Who was the Dakota Sioux chief?

The chief of the Dakota Sioux was Little Crow *(p.62)*.

What was the Dakota Sioux's first treaty about?
The Dakota Sioux signed a treaty with the US Government in 1851. The tribe gave up 24 million acres of land in return for a one-off payment of $1.4 million, plus $80,000 a year in money and resources.

What were the problems with the treaty the Dakota Sioux had signed?
There were several problems with the treaty they had signed:
- Much of the money went straight to traders to whom the tribe was in debt, so the Dakota Sioux only got what was left. When they refused to agree to this, payments were withheld.
- They often ran out of food, as they could not produce enough to last the winter. They went outside of the reservations to hunt and were punished by having more money withheld.
- Food was not sold to them until they agreed to the high prices being set. The only other option was starvation, so they had no option.
- More land was taken from them for settlers.
- The brotherhoods within the tribe often ventured out of the reservation *(p.24)* to raid the locals for resources.

What was the Dakota Sioux's second treaty about?
The second treaty, in 1858, saw the Dakota Sioux sign away another half of their land in return for more money as they were in debt to traders again. Little Crow *(p.62)* was particularly unhappy with this.

What happened to the Dakota Sioux in August 1862?
In August 1862 the Dakota Sioux's crops failed and there was no harvest. The traders refused to give them food on credit. They had no money, as their payment from the government had been delayed. They resorted to trying to eat grass. This led to Little Crow's War *(p.63)*.

What happened to the Dakota Sioux at the Crow Creek Reservation?
After Little Crow's War *(p.63)*, the rest of the Dakota Sioux were moved to Crow Creek Reservation *(p.24)* in South Dakota. The land was dry and barren, and most of them died in their first winter there, in 1863-4.

DID YOU KNOW?

The Dakota Sioux were known for their warrior skills.
They became exceptional at defending their land, fighting with spears and arrows, usually on horseback.

LITTLE CROW'S WAR
Life was hard for the Dakota Sioux, and the land they were given did not live up to government promises.

What was Little Crow's War?
Little Crow's War is the name of an attack by a band of Dakota Sioux *(p.62)*, led by Little Crow *(p.62)*, against the agency in charge of their reservation *(p.24)* and white settlers in the surrounding area.

When was Little Crow's War?
Little Crow's War took place in August 1862.

Why did Little Crow's War happen?
The Dakota Sioux *(p.62)* had been given inferior farm land by the government, which meant their crops failed. The government also failed to make agreed payments to the tribe, leaving them to starve.

What was the result of Little Crow's War?
700 white settlers and soldiers were killed by Little Crow's war band. As a result, the US Army sent soldiers to subdue the Sioux. 300 tribe members were sentenced to death, of whom 38 were hanged. The rest of the tribe was moved to the Crow Creek Reservation *(p.24)*, where many starved. Any of them found outside the reservation were scalped for a bounty.

DID YOU KNOW?

Little Crow escaped at the end of the war, taking 3 white boys as hostages.

One of the hostages was George Washington Ingalls, aged 9. His cousin was Laura Ingalls Wilder, who wrote 'The Little House on the Prairie'.

THE FORT WISE TREATY

US Congress declared that 'Indians should be treated as wards of the state.'

What was the Fort Wise Treaty?
The Fort Wise Treaty was an agreement between the US government and the Cheyenne and Arapaho tribes. The treaty gave the tribes' traditional hunting grounds to the US government, in exchange for $30,000 a year for 15 years, and reservation *(p.24)* land in eastern Colorado.

When was the Fort Wise Treaty signed?
The Fort Wise Treaty was signed in 1861.

Why was the Fort Wise Treaty a problem?
Some of the Cheyenne and Arapaho felt they had not agreed to the treaty, so they did not follow its terms. They were called 'dog soldiers'.

DID YOU KNOW?

The Fort Wise Treaty was hated by the majority of the Cheyenne people.

They argued that it had only been signed by a minority of the Cheyenne chiefs, and without the consent of the rest of the tribe.

DOG SOLDIERS
Young warriors, known as the 'Dog Soldiers', rejected the Fort Wise Treaty.

Who were the Dog Soldiers?
Dog soldiers was the name given to some of the Cheyenne and Arapaho tribes who did not agree with the Fort Wise Treaty *(p.64)* and did not obey the terms. After the Sand Creek Massacre *(p.65)* they killed many white settlers and attacked forts.

DID YOU KNOW?
The Cheyenne word for the dog soldiers was 'Hotamétaneo'o'.

THE CHEYENNE UPRISING
An uprising that came from desperation.

What was the Cheyenne Uprising?
Several Cheyenne groups faced starvation, because they had been given inferior reservation *(p.24)* land in the Treaty of Fort Wise. They turned to attacking wagon trains, to steal food and other supplies.

When did the Cheyenne Uprising happen?
The Cheyenne Uprising took place in 1863.

DID YOU KNOW?
Before the uprising the Cheyenne had turned to eating grass to survive. The reservation's agents showed no sympathy for their plight.

THE SAND CREEK MASSACRE
'Although wrongs have been done me, I live in hopes. I have not got two hearts.'
Black Kettle, speaking about the Sand Creek Massacre

What was the Sand Creek Massacre?
The Sand Creek Massacre was the killing of over 150 Cheyenne and Arapaho by the US Army.

What was Black Kettle's role in the Sand Creek Massacre?
Black Kettle was one of the most important of the Cheyenne leaders. After the Cheyenne Rising he agreed to move his band onto a smaller reservation *(p.24)*. They were camped at Sand Creek.

When was the Sand Creek Massacre?
The Sand Creek Massacre took place on 29th November 1864.

Where was the Sand Creek Massacre?
Sand Creek is in Colorado.

Why did the Sand Creek Massacre take place?
Black Kettle and his band of Cheyenne had moved to Sand Creek under instructions from the US authorities. Black Kettle was flying the white flag of truce on his tipi *(p.21)*. Colonel Chivington *(p.66)* and his 700 cavalry made an unprovoked attack on the settlement.

What were the consequences of the Sand Creek Massacre?
Despite waving the white flag of surrender, 150 Cheyenne men, women and children were killed by the soldiers. Although he was initially praised, when the facts were known, Colonel Chivington *(p.66)* was later forced to resign his post. A new treaty was made, and the tribes were moved to a larger reservation *(p.24)* by the Arkansas River. Payments were promised to survivors of the massacre.

DID YOU KNOW?

The Sand Creek Massacre was later described as 'the foulest and most unjustifiable crime in the annals of America'.
- ✓ Black Kettle survived the massacre.
- ✓ He also saved his wife, who had 9 bullet wounds!

COLONEL CHIVINGTON

'I have come to kill Indians, and believe it is right and honorable to use any means under God's heaven to kill Indians.'
Colonel John Chivington

Who was Colonel Chivington?
Colonel Chivington was a Methodist minister, who served as a colonel in the US Army. He led the attack in the Sand Creek Massacre *(p.65)* of 1864.

RED CLOUD'S WAR
After the government broke its treaty with the Sioux, the Sioux went on the attack.

What was Red Cloud's War?
Red Cloud's War was fought by the Sioux, Cheyenne and Arapaho tribes, against the US Army.

What role did Red Cloud have in the war?
Red Cloud led the Sioux against the US Army during Red Cloud's War. This included inflicting the Fetterman Massacre, which was the most serious defeat of the US Army until the Battle of the Little Bighorn.

When was Red Cloud's War?
Red Cloud's attacks lasted from 1866-1868.

Where was Red Cloud's War?
The attacks happened around the Bozeman Trail in Wyoming.

Why did Red Cloud's War happen?
In 1862 there was Gold Rush *(p.28)* in the Rocky Mountains. The Bozeman Trail was created, leading to new mining towns. Red Cloud believed it was an illegal road, which broke the Fort Laramie Treaty *(p.35)*. The Cheyenne and Arapaho had been moved to a smaller reservation *(p.24)* than they had been promised.

What happened in Red Cloud's War?
The Sioux began attacking travellers on the Bozeman Trail. Peace talks took place, but when the US Army built forts along the Bozeman Trail to protect settlers, Red Cloud walked out. The Sioux then laid siege to the forts and attacked US soldiers. Sitting Bull and Crazy Horse *(p.68)* brought the Cheyenne and Arapaho into the war.

What were the consequences of Red Cloud's War?
The war ended with the Second Fort Laramie Treaty *(p.69)* in 1868.
- The US Army closed the forts on the Bozeman Trail.
- The Great Sioux Reservation *(p.24)* was created.
- The Sioux agreed not to attack travellers, on the condition that no permanent white settlements were built on their land.

> **DID YOU KNOW?**
>
> **Not all the Lakota Sioux agreed with Red Cloud.**
> Some thought it was useless to fight the white settlers. They felt that, by signing the treaty, they would at least get something from the government.

RED CLOUD

'They made us many promises, more than I can remember, but they never kept but one; they promised to take our land, and they took it.'
- saying attributed to Red Cloud

Who was Red Cloud?
Red Cloud *(p.66)* was one of the most important Lakota Sioux leaders of the 19th century. He was a brilliant general and inflicted many defeats on the US Army. After the war, he led his people in the transition to the reservations.

CRAZY HORSE

A determined man who fought for his tribe's rights.

Who was Crazy Horse?

Crazy Horse was a famous Sioux leader, who fought for his tribe's right to move freely on the land. He led the Oglala Sioux at the Battle of the Little Bighorn. He surrendered to the US Army in 1877, and was killed while resisting imprisonment later that year.

SITTING BULL

A brave chief who managed to gain many victories for his people.

Who was Sitting Bull?

Sitting Bull was a Sioux leader, who united his men against the US Army. He led the Lakota Sioux and Northern Cheyenne during the Battle of the Little Bighorn. He was killed by reservation *(p.24)* police officers in 1890.

FETTERMAN'S TRAP

A trap, orchestrated by a group of Native Americans, sprung on a troop of soldiers led by Captain Fetterman

What was Fetterman's Trap?

Fetterman's Trap, also known as the Fetterman Massacre, occurred during Red Cloud's War *(p.66)*. It was an attack by a group of Native Americans *(p.17)*, on US soldiers led by Captain Fetterman.

When was Fetterman's Trap?

The soldiers were killed on 21st December 1866.

What happened at Fetterman's Trap?

A party of woodcutters was attacked, near Fort Phil Kearny, by a party of Sioux. As they had anticipated, a detachment of soldiers left the fort to protect the woodcutters. Many more Native Americans *(p.17)* ambushed them and killed 81 soldiers, before blocking the route to the fort, rendering it unusable.

What were the consequences of Fetterman's Trap?

The Second Fort Laramie Treaty *(p.69)* was negotiated, which brought peace to the region for eight years.

DID YOU KNOW?

The Native Americans made sure the American soldiers were dead.

After the battle they stripped and scalped the American soldiers, then mutilated their bodies.

THE SECOND FORT LARAMIE TREATY, 1868

A treaty that guaranteed Arapaho, Dakota and Lakota tribes possession of some parts of the Dakota territory

What was the Second Fort Laramie Treaty?
The Second Fort Laramie Treaty was an agreement signed after the failure of the first Fort Laramie Treaty *(p.35)*. It was signed by the Lakota and Dakota Sioux *(p.62)*, the Arapaho, and the US government.

When was the second Fort Laramie Treaty signed?
The treaty was signed in 1868.

What were the terms of the Second Fort Laramie Treaty?
The second Fort Laramie Treaty ensured peace between the Native Americans *(p.17)* and the settlers. There were a number of terms to the treaty.
- The US Army closed the forts on the Bozeman Trail.
- The Great Sioux Reservation *(p.24)* was created, which included the sacred Black Hills.
- The Sioux agreed not to attack travellers, on the condition that no permanent white settlements were built on their land.
- It gave the US government the authority to punish anyone who broke the treaty.

> **DID YOU KNOW?**
>
> **The Government eventually broke the terms of the treaty.**
> When the Black Hills gold rush started, more and more white settlers moved into the sacred lands of the Sioux. The US government did nothing to stop them.

DRY FARMING

A technique established to solve old problems.

What was dry farming?
Dry farming was a technique that trapped rainwater under the ground's surface in areas where there was little flowing water.

Who invented dry farming?
Hardy Webster Campbell developed the technique of dry farming.

Where was dry farming used?
It was first used in Dakota but became popular in many homesteader *(p.46)* areas across the Great Plains.

When was dry farming invented?
This farming technique was first used in 1879.

> **DID YOU KNOW?**
>
> Hardy Webster Campbell created the technique of dry farming and demonstrated it to other farmers.

THE SEED DRILL

An ancient technique used to fix an old problem.

What is a seed drill?

A seed drill was used to plant seeds deep in the ground. This was needed in the west as the ground was so dry. The drills were drawn by horses, and seeds were planted automatically.

THE CATTLE INDUSTRY IN THE 1880S

A way to make a quick buck.

What was the cattle industry like in the 1880s?

By the 1880s, the cattle industry *(p.53)* had flourished to a point of overstocking itself.

What were the consequences of overstocking of the cattle industry in the 1880s?

There were several consequences to overstocking the cattle:

- So much beef was available the price of cattle dropped.
- Droughts and prairie fires left grass in short supply for the many cattle that needed it for food.
- The Great Die-up *(p.71)*. The exceptionally severe winter of 1886-87 saw thousands of cattle die as they could not eat the grass through the snow.
- Many ranchers started to farm smaller areas to enable them to keep cattle alive in the severe winters. They fenced the ranches off for protection.
- Quality of beef became important, and many ranchers switched to Hereford or Holstein cattle, which were considered 'pure breeds'.

> **DID YOU KNOW?**
>
> **New cow breeds were introduced.**
> Some cattleman tried to breed the extinct buffalo alongside cows to see what would happen. It was mostly unsuccessful, but there was a successful cross between the Texas Longhorn and India's Brahman cow.

THE GREAT DIE-UP
The harsh winter of 1886-87 was known as the Great (or Big) Die-up.

What was the Great Die-up?
The Great Die-up happened during a particularly harsh winter when the cattle could not access grass through the snow. Many thousands of animals died, thought to be up to 15% of the total number. Many people in the cattle industry *(p.53)* went bankrupt as a result.

When was the Great Die-up?
The Great Die-up happened in the winter of 1886-87.

What was the impact of the Great Die-up on the cattle industry?
After the Great Die-up, there were 15% fewer cattle. This led to some ranches going bankrupt. Smaller ones survived by enclosing their lands and cattle, in order to monitor them better. Ranches also switched to purer breeds of cattle.

What was the impact of the Great Die Up on cowboys?
There were fewer jobs available for cowboys. Many worked on the smaller ranches, patrolling and maintaining fences, and feeding and monitoring the cattle.

> **DID YOU KNOW?**
> **It took ages for farmers to see the extent of the damage.**
> Cattle skeletons were spread across the fields and rivers.

THE EXODUSTER MOVEMENT
Due to extreme persecution from white southerners, many African Americans moved westwards to seek new opportunities.

What was the Exoduster Movement?
After the abolition of slavery, following the Civil War, many African Americans chose to move westwards to seek a new life. They moved to areas such as Kansas, Indiana, Illinois and Missouri.

Who started the Exoduster Movement?
Benjamin Singleton *(p.72)* is credited with starting the movement.

When was the Exoduster Movement?
The movement started in 1873 and became large scale by 1879.

How many emigrated during the Exoduster Movement?
40,000 black settlers had moved by the end of 1879.

Why did the Exoduster Movement happen?
There were several reasons for this mass migration of black settlers:
- Benjamin Singleton *(p.72)*, who settled in Kansas in 1873, promoted the idea through newspapers and at meetings that others should follow him.
- Henry Adams *(p.73)* also promoted the idea of black migration for a new life. He also promoted the idea of migration to Liberia.
- Many black Americans trusted the word of God, and believed God would provide for them.
- The Homesteader *(p.46)* Act made it possible for many poor people to make a new start.
- Kansas was a 'free state' by 1861, which meant it was free of slavery. This made it very appealing.
- After the Civil War, freed slaves wanted new jobs and a better way of life, wherever they could find it.

What was the impact of the Exoduster Movement?
The exodus of so many people had a number of results:
- New settlements were founded, such as Nicodemus in Kansas. By 1880, more than 43,000 African Americans had settled in Kansas.
- Much of the available land was difficult to farm.
- Many of the black settlers could not afford the administration fees needed to gain land through the Homesteaders Act.
- Many white Americans opposed the migration and believed the black settlers should not be helped. Many felt they should be sent back to the southern states.
- By the end of the 1880s many of the settlers were better prepared for migration, so a lot of the earlier issues resolved themselves. However, black settlers in Kansas did remain poorer than white ones.
- The movement triggered similar movements of black settlers to other areas, such as to Nebraska and Oklahoma.

> **DID YOU KNOW?**
>
> **The Exoduster Movement's importance is understated.**
> - ✓ It was the first voluntary movement of black people from one place to another, rather than them being forcibly removed.
> - ✓ It served as a stepping stone for many African Americans to strike out and gain their own independence and freedom.

BENJAMIN SINGLETON
Benjamin Singleton is known as the 'father of the African American exodus'.

Who was Benjamin Singleton?
Benjamin Singleton started the Exoduster Movement *(p.71)*. He even declared, 'I am the whole cause of the Kansas immigration.' After settling in Kansas in 1873, he promoted the idea that others should follow him.

HENRY ADAMS
An ex-slave from Louisiana who had big idea.

Who was Henry Adams?
Henry Adams promoted the idea of black migration for a new life in the western states of America after the Civil War. He also promoted the idea of migration to Liberia, in West Africa.

THE OKLAHOMA LAND RUSH
New, cheap territory was opened up, and many made a mad dash for it.

What was the Oklahoma Rush?
At the end of the Plains Wars, the western territories became states of the USA. The government opened up these new lands for settlement. The first area was Oklahoma, and the land grab there became known as the Oklahoma Land Rush.

Who was involved in the Oklahoma Land Rush?
White settlers were allowed onto this section of land by the US government, making Oklahoma available for homestead claims. White settlers rushed in, and took land from the Native Americans *(p.17)*.

Where did the Oklahoma Land Rush happen?
The land that was opened to settlement for the white settlers included all or part of Cleveland, Kingfisher, Logan, and Oklahoma.

When was Oklahoma Land Rush?
The Oklahoma Land Rush began on the 22nd April 1889, in Central Oklahoma, USA.

Why was the Oklahoma Land Rush significant?
The Oklahoma Land Rush was significant as another example of how the US government gave away Native American *(p.17)* land, due to pressure and demands from white settlers.

> **DID YOU KNOW?**
> It is estimated that around 2 million acres of land opened up in Oklahoma.

SHARECROPPERS
An opportunity that seemed like freedom but often wasn't.

What were sharecroppers?
Sharecroppers were former slaves turned farmers. The landowner supplied housing and tools, while the sharecroppers grew the crops and were allowed to keep a share of what they produced. They were not treated well by their white employers, and were always in debt.

> **DID YOU KNOW?**
>
> **Sharecropping was, in effect, just another term for slavery.**
> Sharecroppers did not have great way of life. They often still lived in poverty, and often found themselves in deep debt to the landowners.

BILLY THE KID
'I wasn't the leader of any gang. I was Billy all the time.'
Billy the Kid to a Las Vegas reporter, following his capture in 1880

Who was Billy the Kid?
Billy the Kid was a famous outlaw and gunfighter of the American West. His real name was Henry McCarty.

When was Billy the Kid born?
Billy the Kid was born in 1859.

When did Billy the Kid die?
Billy the Kid died in 1881.

What was Billy the Kid's early life like?
Billy the Kid grew up in a mining camp in New Mexico. He got into trouble when he was 14 or 15 years old for stealing, and graduated to horse *(p.19)* theft and cattle rustling.

Why is Billy the Kid famous?
Billy the Kid is famous for frequently escaping jail after after being arrested for stealing cattle or horses.

How was Billy the Kid involved in the Lincoln County War?
Billy the Kid fought for cattle baron *(p.58)* John Chisum *(p.76)* in the Lincoln County War *(p.75)*.

What was Billy the Kid's personal war?
Billy the Kid vowed to murder whoever was responsible for the death of his friend, Henry Tunstall, in the Lincoln County War *(p.75)*.

What was Billy the Kid's link to Pat Garrett?
Billy the Kid became so notorious that when Pat Garrett *(p.76)* was elected sheriff in Lincoln County, his main job was to bring him to justice. Garrett tracked Billy down, imprisoned him, and took him to court. When Billy escaped, Garrett tracked him down again and shot him dead.

 ### Why were there people like Billy the Kid in the West?
There were several reasons why people like Billy the Kid and many others turned to lawlessness in the American West:

- Poverty was such a problem that many people saw stealing as the only way they could survive.
- With so many settlers in some areas, conflicts arose over the limited resources available. This led to many acts of lawlessness.
- There were too many lawless people, which triggered fear in others and led them to wanting to defend themselves. In turn, their own behaviour became more lawless.
- Settlers often felt independent of America as a whole, so not subject to the country's laws.

 ### How did Billy the Kid and others get away with their lawlessness?
There were 4 main reasons Billy the Kid and others could get away with their lawless behaviour.

- The territories were so large, and law officials so few, that there were many places outlaws could hide easily.
- There was a lot of corruption. People like Billy the Kid could often get away with breaking the law by paying off officials.
- There were not enough law officers, or people who wanted to be law officers.
- There was also a real risk that if a law officer captured a criminal, others would try to release them and lynch the law officer.

 ### What problems of law and order does the story of Billy the Kid demonstrate?
The case of Billy the Kid demonstrates a number of problems with law and order *(p.38)* in the American West:

- The helplessness of people against big businesses could lead to lawlessness, as the only way they could stand up to the rich and powerful.
- Many acts of lawlessness were committed by gunmen hired by the cattle barons, or by others who wanted the barons' land and resources.
- The justice system was weak and corrupt, so unable to bring lawless people to justice.

DID YOU KNOW?

Although it seems he had a long life due to the string of crimes he committed, Billy the Kid was only 21 when he died.

THE LINCOLN COUNTY WAR
A war between competing cattle barons and ranchers.

 ### What was the Lincoln County War?
The Lincoln County War of 1878-1881 was fought over the control of profits from the cattle business. The main factions were led by cattle baron *(p.58)* John Chisum *(p.76)* and businessman Lawrence Murphy *(p.76)*.

JOHN CHISUM
A cattle baron who became a prominent figure in the Lincoln County War.

Who was John Chisum?
John Chisum was a cattle baron *(p.58)* who owned a large ranch *(p.59)* in New Mexico. He took part in the Lincoln County War *(p.75)* of 1878-1881.

MURPHY
A prominent rancher who became involved in the Lincoln County War

Who was Lawrence Murphy?
Lawrence Murphy was a businessman who was involved in the Lincoln County War *(p.75)* of 1878-1881.

PAT GARRETT
'The tall slayer of Billy the Kid, and without question the American West's most famous lawman after that deed.'
Leon Metz, historian, writing about Pat Garrett

Who was Pat Garrett?
Pat Garrett was a sheriff who, when elected, was given the job of bringing Billy the Kid *(p.74)* to justice. Garrett tracked him down, imprisoned him, and took him to court. When Billy escaped, Garrett found him again and shot him dead.

WYATT EARP
'No wise man ever took a handgun to a gunfight.'
Wyatt Earp

Who was Wyatt Earp?
Wyatt Earp was a lawman in the American West from May 1874.

How did Earp become a lawman?
Earp helped a local deputy marshal when some cowboys got too rowdy in Wichita. He was then offered a job as deputy marshal by the mayor.

What jobs did Earp have?
After starting as deputy marshal in Wichita, Earp became marshal of Dodge City. He was later the deputy sheriff of Tombstone.

What happened to Earp in Tombstone?
In 1880 Earp was employed by the rich businessmen of Tombstone to recover stolen property - cowboys had been stealing mules and horses, and robbing stagecoaches. This was the start of a long feud between the cowboys and Earp and his brothers.

What happened to Earp at the OK Corral?
On 26th October, 1881, Earp and his brothers - Virgil and Morgan - exchanged gunfire with the Clantons and McLaurys. The Earps killed Tom and Frank McLaury, along with Billy *(p.74)* Clanton, during the gunfight.

How did the feud with Earp and the others end?
Virgil Earp was shot in 1881, and Morgan Earp was shot and killed in 1882. Wyatt Earp then shot 2 men he believed were responsible for the killing, but the public saw him as a lawless murderer. He and his family were forced to leave Tombstone.

> **DID YOU KNOW?**
>
> **Wyatt Earp has become a widely recognised figure in popular history.**
> - ✔ There have been dozens of films, TV series and books about his life.
> - ✔ He was first portrayed in film in 1923 - 6 years before he died! Earp worked as a technical consultant on the film.

THE JOHNSON COUNTY WAR
The War on Powder River

What was the Johnson County War?
The Johnson County War was a conflict over the ownership and use of the 'range' (the wide open plains).

When was the Johnson County War?
The Johnson County War took place in 1892.

Why was the Johnson County War significant?
The Johnson County War was significant because it showed that lawlessness continued into the 1890s.

Why did the Johnson County War happen?
Tensions in Wyoming laid the foundations. Small ranchers were fed up with the way larger, rich businesses held all the power. The larger ranchers accused the smaller ones of stealing their cattle after a harsh winter in 1886. Juries, made up of locals, never convicted the larger ranchers. The Wyoming Stock Growers' Association *(p.79)* - the WSGA - also added to the tension.

What happened in the Johnson County War?
The WSGA *(p.79)* planned an invasion of Johnson County, seeking to kill 70 men it believed the county could 'do without'.

How was the Johnson County War paid for?
The WSGA *(p.79)* raised over $100,000 from the rich businessmen of the area.

Who was involved in the Johnson County War?
The WGSA hired 22 Texas gunmen.

Was the Johnson County War a success?
The invasion failed because the Texas gunmen attacked a local ranch *(p.59)* and shot Nate Champion. He was one of the men identified by the WSGA *(p.79)* to be killed, but they burned his house to smoke him out. This outraged the locals, who wanted to protect their own properties. Sheriff Angus surrounded the invaders at the TA Ranch until the US 6th Cavalry arrived and saved them.

What happened at the trial after the Johnson County War?
The trial of the Texas gunmen resulted in the charges against them being dropped. There were several reasons for this:
- ☑ The Governor of Wyoming was a friend of the invaders and the WSGA *(p.79)*.
- ☑ The WSGA *(p.79)* hired the best Chicago lawyers to defend them.
- ☑ The lawyers successfully argued the gunmen would not receive a fair trial in Johnson Country and proceedings were moved to Cheyenne.
- ☑ The lawyers made sure proceedings dragged on for a long time. They knew the Johnson County prosecutors would run out of money and would have to end the trial.

> **DID YOU KNOW?**
> You can still visit TA Ranch, where the Texas gunmen were pinned down.

ELLA WATSON AND JIM AVERILL
Two small ranch owners who succumbed to a terrible fate

Who were Ella Watson and Jim Averill?
Watson and Averill were homesteaders. Their homestead was in the middle of a large, open-range pasture used by cattleman Albert Bothwell.

What happened to Watson and Averill?
Watson was accused of stealing cattle from Bothwell. She denied this. Watson and Averill were both hanged by Bothwell and his men. Bothwell then took their land and cattle for himself.

> **DID YOU KNOW?**
> **It was rumoured Watson and Averill were married.**
> Watson, however, kept her surname so she could get land from the Homestead Act; it gave land to single women but not married ones.

THE WYOMING STOCK GROWERS' ASSOCIATION
Started in 1872, it gained great influence throughout the American West.

Who were the WSGA?
The Wyoming Stock Growers' Association (WSGA) was a group of ranchers who worked to eliminate cattle rustling during the annual cattle round-up. Many of the 'alleged' rustlers were smaller ranch *(p.59)* owners who were competing with the big ranchers for land, water, and livestock. The WSGA planned and started the Johnson County War *(p.77)*.

> **DID YOU KNOW?**
> The WSGA still exists today.

THE BATTLE OF LITTLE BIGHORN (1876)
A victory for the North Plains Indians, which ultimately led to their defeat.

What was the Battle of Little Bighorn?
The Battle of the Little Bighorn took place at the Little Bighorn River, in Montana Territory.

Who fought in the Battle of the Little Bighorn?
The Battle of the Little Bighorn was fought between an alliance of Sioux, Cheyenne and some Arapaho, against the US Federal Army commanded by George Armstrong Custer *(p.81)*.

When was the Battle of the Little Bighorn?
The Battle of the Little Bighorn took place on 25th and 26th June, 1876.

What were the causes of the Battle of Little Bighorn?
There were 4 main reasons for the Battle of the Little Bighorn.

- In 1875, gold was discovered in the Black Hills of South Dakota. This led to an influx of gold miners, which broke the Second Fort Laramie Treaty *(p.69)*. The US Government did nothing to stop the prospectors.
- The US Government offered to buy the Black Hills from the Sioux. As this was sacred land, the Sioux refused.
- In December 1875, Sioux and Cheyenne people refused an order from the US Government to return to their reservations. Instead, they joined Sitting Bull and Crazy Horse *(p.68)* in Montana.
- Some Sioux began attacking the miners and other settlers. The US Army was sent to the area to protect the settlers, and to force the Sioux and Cheyenne back to their reservations.

What happened at the Battle of the Little Bighorn?
There were several key events at the Battle of the Little Bighorn.

- On 25th June, Custer discovered a Sioux village. He also spotted a nearby group of around forty warriors, and attacked them before they could alert the main party. However, Custer was unaware that the warriors in the village vastly outnumbered his force.
- The Sioux and Cheyenne crossed the river together, meeting the advancing soldiers and forcing them back. At the same time another force, commanded by Crazy Horse *(p.68)*, surrounded Custer and his men. They began the attack with heavy gun- and arrow-fire.

- As the Native Americans *(p.17)* closed in on Custer, he ordered his men to shoot their horses, and stack their bodies up to form a protective barrier. This, however, did little to protect his troops from the enemy bullets.
- Custer and his men were killed in less than an hour. It was the worst military disaster America had seen.

Why was Custer defeated at the Battle of the Little Bighorn?

There were 9 key reasons for the defeat of Custer at the Battle of the Little Bighorn.

- Custer was arrogant and over-confident. He wanted a victory to bolster his political ambitions (as he was considering running for president).
- Even though he was told to wait for support, Custer ignored orders and acted alone.
- Custer force-marched his men through the mountains, instead of going around them. By the time he arrived, his troops and their horses were exhausted.
- Custer divided his force into three groups. Although this was a standard US Army tactic, it weakened his already outnumbered force.
- Custer did not know how big the Sioux army was, or how well armed the warriors were. He had poor and incorrect information.
- He was vastly outnumbered. There were up to 1,500 Sioux warriors against around 250 US troops.
- He expected the Sioux to scatter and run. Instead, they outmanoeuvred and surrounded him.
- Crazy Horse *(p.68)* and other Sioux leaders were talented and experienced commanders.
- The Sioux fought with determination and desperation, as they regarded the battle as their last chance to defeat the US.

Why was the Battle of Little Bighorn important?

Little Bighorn showed the Native Americans *(p.17)* power: they had achieved their greatest victory. However, outraged over the death of a popular Civil War leader, the US government fought back.

What were the consequences of the Battle of the Little Bighorn?

Despite their victory, the Battle of Little Bighorn had 5 main consequences for the Sioux nations and Plains Indians *(p.17)* as a whole.

- Once news spread that more than 250 US soldiers had been killed by the Sioux, public opinion quickly turned against the Native Americans *(p.17)*.
- Plains Indians *(p.17)* had to stay on their reservations. Any found outside their reservations were pursued by the army and killed. By the early 1880s, almost all Cheyenne and Sioux were confined to reservations, totally dependent on the US government for food and shelter.
- Previous treaties were now ignored. The government decided that Native Americans *(p.17)* had forfeited the rights to have any special treatment, and started to eliminate Native American culture.
- The Sioux were forced to sell the Black Hills, and their reservations were split up.
- To prevent any future Sioux attacks their weapons and horses were taken. New forts were built, and the number of soldiers in the area increased.

DID YOU KNOW?

No-one knows what happened to Custer's body, although there have been different rumours.
- ✓ Some say he was scalped.
- ✓ Others say that his body was ripped apart, and that his ear drums were pierced because he had refused to listen to the Native Americans.

GENERAL GEORGE ARMSTRONG CUSTER

A highly regarded general who had big ambitions

Who was George Armstrong Custer?

George Armstrong Custer was a United States Army officer. He served as a cavalry commander in the American Civil War *(p.40)* and the American Indian Wars.

What was George Armstrong Custer's role in the Indian Wars?

After the American Civil War *(p.40)* he pursued US aims in the West, and participated in a campaign against the Sioux and Cheyenne Indians. He spent the next few years in many skirmishes with the Plains Indians *(p.17)*, and developed the view that they were savages.

What was George Armstrong Custer's Black Hills expedition?

Custer led the Black Hills expedition for the United States Army. Its mission was to look for suitable locations for a fort, to find a route to the southwest, and to investigate the possibility of mining for gold. Gold was found in the Black Hills, which prompted a gold rush *(p.28)*. This, in turn, antagonised the Sioux, as their sacred land had been protected by treaties with the US government.

What did George Armstrong Custer do in the Battle of Little Bighorn?

Custer led the 7th Cavalry in a disastrous attack against the largest gathering of Plains Indians *(p.17)* ever seen. He was killed at the Battle of the Little Bighorn, in what became known as 'Custer's Last Stand.'.

What legacy did George Armstrong Custer leave?

Custer was given a hero's burial at West Point. Owing to his status as a Civil War hero, his death shocked the American people. As Americans came to regret their government's mistreatment of Native Americans *(p.17)*, however, Custer's image changed.

> **DID YOU KNOW?**
>
> **Custer used cinnamon oil on his hair.**
> ✓ Custer took his looks very seriously, and wore elaborate uniforms.
> ✓ He used cinnamon oil on his hair, to make his blond locks glossy.

WOUNDED KNEE

The final battle between Sioux Indians and the US Army. Its significance lives on today.

What was the Wounded Knee Massacre?

The Battle of Wounded Knee (or the Wounded Knee Massacre) was the final battle in the wars between the US Army and the Sioux.

Who was involved in the Battle of Wounded Knee?

The Battle of Wounded Knee was between the Sioux Indians, led by 'Big Foot', and the 7th US Cavalry.

When was the Battle of Wounded Knee?
The Battle of Wounded Knee happened on the 29th December 1890.

Where did the Battle of Wounded Knee take place?
The Battle of Wounded Knee took place at Wounded Knee Creek on the Lakota Pine Ridge Indian Reservation *(p.24)*, in the US state of South Dakota.

What happened at the Battle of Wounded Knee?
The US Cavalry were sent to disarm the Sioux and arrest their leader, Big Foot. One of them resisted, and the soldiers opened fire. Over 250 Sioux and 25 troopers were killed.

> **DID YOU KNOW?**
>
> **Wounded Knee began as a scuffle, when the firing of one shot led to a massacre.**
> - The US soldiers opened fire on Sioux Indians, shooting as many men, woman and children as possible.
> - The massacre lives on in the memory of Native Americans of all tribes.
> - There was no inquiry into what happened - in fact, the soldiers were given medals, and the public expressed approval of the way they had conducted themselves.

THE GHOST DANCE
A way for the Native Americans to regain what had been taken from them.

What was the Ghost Dance?
The Ghost Dance was a new religious movement among the Native Americans *(p.17)*, which incorporated many of their traditional beliefs.

When did the Ghost Dance begin?
The Ghost Dance began on January 1st 1889, during a solar eclipse.

Who started the Ghost Dance?
The Ghost Dance was started by a Native American *(p.17)* holy man called Wovoka.

Why did Native Americans do the Ghost Dance?
Many Native Americans *(p.17)* believed they had angered the gods by abandoning their culture, which had caused their misfortunes and defeat. They practised the Ghost Dance as a way of making amends, in the hope that the gods would create a new world for them.

What did Native Americans believe about the Ghost Dance?
Native Americans *(p.17)* believed that the Ghost Dance religion would do 4 main things.
- It would bring an end to white settlement in America.

- ✅ The buffalo *(p.20)* would return.
- ✅ Their ancestors would come back to life.
- ✅ Their traditional way of life would be restored.

What were the consequences of the Ghost Dance?

The Ghost Dance worried the US Government, who tried to ban the religion. This led to the 'Ghost Dance War', which ended at Wounded Knee.

> **DID YOU KNOW?**
>
> **Many hoped that the Ghost Dance would banish the European settlers.**
> - ✓ The practice of the Ghost Dance spread throughout the West, even up to the Canadian border.
> - ✓ The Native Americans hoped to get their land back, and that the buffalo (which had been hunted almost to extinction) would return.

THE DAWES ACT

The Dawes Act provided a way to give white settlers more land.

❓ What was the Dawes Act?

The Dawes Act was a law which distributed Indian reservation *(p.24)* land to individual Native American *(p.17)* families. They were given a plot of land, with the intention that they would become self-sufficient farmers.

👤 Who authorised the Dawes Act?

President Grover Cleveland authorised the confiscation and redistribution of Native American *(p.17)* lands.

⏳ When did the Dawes Act become law?

The Dawes Act was enacted in February 1887.

 Why was the Dawes Act created?

The objective of the act was to:
- ✅ Further encourage Native Americans *(p.17)* to integrate into white American society.
- ✅ Free up more land for white settlers.

What were the effects of the Dawes Act?

The Dawes Act helped to further destroy Native American *(p.17)* culture.
- ✅ It undermined the tribal structure of Native Americans *(p.17)*, as they were now citizens of the USA.
- ✅ It eliminated the need to hunt buffalo *(p.20)*.
- ✅ It eroded Native American *(p.17)* spiritual beliefs, which were often focused on their culture and tribal structure. Some Native Americans became Christians.

DID YOU KNOW?

The provisions of the Dawes Act were only available to some Native American tribes.

They were not available to Cherokee, Creek, Choctaw, Chickasaw, Seminole, Miami, Peoria, the Osage, Sac, and Fox in the Oklahoma Territory. Nor were they available to the reservations occupied by Seneca Nation of New York. The list goes on!

THE CLOSURE OF THE FRONTIER
A danger for Native Americans, but a chance of freedom for the settlers.

What was the closure of the frontier?

In 1890, the US Census Bureau closed the frontier. The West had been fully settled so the frontier had, in effect, ceased to exist.

What was the impact of the closure of the frontier?

There were 3 main consequences of the frontier closure.

- ☑ The preservation of wild areas, which later resulted in national parks such as Yellowstone and Yosemite.
- ☑ Manifest Destiny had, officially, been achieved.
- ☑ The frontier had represented danger because of the Native Americans *(p.17)* who lived in the region. This was no longer the case.

DID YOU KNOW?

The closing of the frontier was seen as very significant event in American history.

- ✓ At the time it offered many European settlers an opportunity to start a new life.
- ✓ However, it had a detrimental impact on Native Americans: the forced migration to reservations, the impact of the wars, and many deaths from European diseases.

GLOSSARY

A

Abolition - the act of abolishing something, i.e. to stop or get rid of it.

Agriculture - an umbrella term to do with farming, growing crops or raising animals.

Alliance - a union between groups or countries that benefits each member.

B

Bankrupt - to be insolvent; to have run out of resources with which to pay existing debts.

Blasphemy - the act of speaking insultingly about or with lack of reverence for God or sacred objects.

Blockade - a way of blocking or sealing an area to prevent goods, supplies or people from entering or leaving. It often refers to blocking transport routes.

Bribe, Bribery, Bribes - to dishonestly persuade someone to do something for you in return for money or other inducements.

C

Campaign - a political movement to get something changed; in military terms, it refers to a series of operations to achieve a goal.

Cavalry - the name given to soldiers who fight on horseback.

Claim - someone's assertion of their right to something - for example, a claim to the throne.

Communal - referring to something that is shared by all members of a community, be it an action or possession etc.

Conscription - mandatory enlistment of people into a state service, usually the military.

Corrupt - when someone is willing to act dishonestly for their own personal gain.

Council - an advisory or administrative body set up to manage the affairs of a place or organisation. The Council of the League of Nations contained the organisation's most powerful members.

Coup - a sudden, violent and illegal overthrow of the government by a small group - for example, the chiefs of an army.

Culture - the ideas, customs, and social behaviour of a particular people or society.

Currency - an umbrella term for any form of legal tender, but most commonly referring to money.

D

Debt - when something, usually money, is owed by a person, organisation or institution to another.

Deport - to expel someone from a country and, usually, return them to their homeland.

Disarm - to remove any land, sea and air weaponry.

Dispute - a disagreement or argument; often used to describe conflict between different countries.

E

Economic - relating to the economy; also used when justifying something in terms of profitability.

Economy - a country, state or region's position in terms of production and consumption of goods and services, and the supply of money.

Export - to transport goods for sale to another country.

Extreme - furthest from the centre or any given point. If someone holds extreme views, they are not moderate and are considered radical.

F

Famine - a severe food shortage resulting in starvation and death, usually the result of bad harvests.

Fasting - to deliberately refrain from eating, and often drinking, for a period of time.

Fatalities, Fatality - Deaths.

Federal - in US politics this means 'national', referring to the whole country rather than any individual state.

Frontier - a line or border between two areas.

G

Guerrilla tactics, Guerrilla warfare - a way of fighting that typically involves hit-and-run style tactics.

H

Harvest - the process of gathering and collecting crops.

I

Immigrant - someone who moves to another country.

Immigration - the act of coming to a foreign country with the intention of living there permanently.

Independence, Independent - to be free of control, often meaning by another country, allowing the people of a nation the ability to govern themselves.

Industrialisation, Industrialise, Industrialised - the process of developing industry in a country or region where previously there was little or none.

Industry - the part of the economy concerned with turning raw materials into into manufactured goods, for example making furniture from wood.

Inferior - lower in rank, status or quality.

Inflation - the general increase in the prices of goods which means money does not buy as much as it used to.

Integrate - to bring people or groups with specific characteristics

GLOSSARY

or needs into equal participation with others; to merge one thing with another to form a single entity.

Investor - someone who puts money into something with the expectation of future profit.

J

Juries, Jury - a group of people sworn to listen to evidence on a legal case and then deliver an impartial verdict based on what they have heard.

L

Lynch, Lynched, Lynching - the killing of someone by a group of people for an alleged offence without a legal trial, usually publicly and often by hanging.

M

Manifest destiny - the belief white Americans had the God-given right to expand westwards across North America.

Mass - an act of worship in the Catholic Church.

Massacre - the deliberate and brutal slaughter of many people.

Mechanisation - Where human workers are replaced by machines or robots.

Militia - an army created from the general population.

Mine - an explosive device usually hidden underground or underwater.

Minister - a senior member of government, usually responsible for a particular area such as education or finance.

N

New World - the name given in the 16th century to describe the Americas and the Caribbean, distinguishing it from the 'Old World', which referred to Europe.

P

Persecute - to treat someone unfairly because of their race, religion or political beliefs.

Persecution - hostility towards or harassment of someone, usually due to their race, religion or political beliefs.

Pioneer - the first person to explore or settle in a new area.

Polygamy - the practise of being married to more than one person at the same time.

Population - the number of people who live in a specified place.

Poverty - the state of being extremely poor.

Prejudice - prejudgement - when you assume something about someone based on a feature like their religion or skin colour, rather than knowing it as fact.

President - the elected head of state of a republic.

Prevent, Preventative, Preventive - steps taken to stop something from happening.

Printing press - a machine that reproduces writing and images by using ink on paper, making many identical copies.

Production - a term used to describe how much of something is made, for example saying a factory has a high production rate.

Profit - generally refers to financial gain; the amount of money made after deducting buying, operating or production costs.

Prospector - someone who searches for gold.

Q

Quarantine - a period of isolation where a person or animal who has or may have a communicable disease is kept away from others.

R

Raid - a quick surprise attack on the enemy.

Refugee, Refugees - a person who has been forced to leave where they live due to war, disaster or persecution.

Reservation - an area of land given to Native Americans by the US government to keep them away from settlers.

Riots - violent disturbances involving a crowd of people.

Rustling - Rustling is the stealing of livestock.

S

Secede, Secession - formal withdrawal from a larger entity, such as 11 states leaving the United States prior to the American Civil War.

Sharecropper - someone who farmed land belonging to a landowner in return for giving them a share of their crops.

Sheriff, Sheriffs - an important royal official in medieval England, responsible for running the local court and ensuring tax was paid to the monarch.

Siege - action by enemy forces to surround a place or building, cutting off access and supplies, with the aim of either destroying it, gaining entry, or starving the inhabitants out.

Sod - the surface of the ground, often mud, on which grass is growing.

State, States - an area of land or a territory ruled by one government.

T

Tactic - a strategy or method of achieving a goal.

Terrain - a stretch of land and usually used to refer to its physical features, eg mountainous, jungle etc.

Territories, Territory - an area of land under the control of a ruler/country.

Treaty - a formal agreement, signed and ratified by two or more parties.

W

Ward, Wards - A ward is someone who is taken under the protection and power of someone else, usually because it is believed that they do not have the capacity to know what is best for them.

INDEX

A
Abilene - 51
Adams, Henry - 73
American Civil War - 40
Averill, Jim - 78

B
Barbed wire - 48
Battle of Little Big Horn - 79
Billy the Kid - 74
Black Kettle - 65
Brigham Young - 33
Buffalo and the Native Americans - 20

C
California Gold Rush - 28
Cattle baron - 58
Cattle industry - 53
Cattle industry in 1880s - 70
Cattle trails - 57
Charles Goodnight - 56
Cheyenne Uprising - 65
Chisholm Trail - 55
Chisum, John - 76
Chivington, Colonel - 66
Closure of the Frontier - 84
Cow towns - 50
Cowboys - 58
Crazy Horse - 68
Custer, George Armstrong - 81

D
Dakota Sioux - 62
Daniel Halladay - 47
Dawes Act, 1887 - 83
Dog soldiers - 65
Donner Party - 29
Dry farming - 69

E
Earp, Wyatt - 76
Exoduster movement - 71

F
Fetterman's Trap - 68
First Fort Laramie Treaty, 1851 - 35
First Indian Appropriations Act, 1851 - 24
Fort Laramie Treaty, 1851 - 35
Fort Laramie Treaty, 1868 - 69
Fort Wise Treaty, 1861 - 64
Fremont, John - 28
Frontier, closure - 84

G
Garrett, Pat - 76
George Armstrong Custer - 81
Ghost Dance - 82
Goodnight, Charles - 56
Goodnight-Loving Trail - 55
Great American Desert - 16
Great Die-Up - 71
Great Plains Settlements in 1850s - 33
Great Salt Lake - 32

H
Halladay, Daniel - 47
Hell on Wheels - 50
Hickok, Wild Bill - 52
Homestead Act, 1862 - 41
Homesteaders - 46
Horses and the Native Americans - 19

I
Iliff, John - 57
Indian Appropriations Act, 1851 - 24
Indian Appropriations Act, 1871 - 62
Indian Removal Act, 1830 - 22
Indian Trade and Intercourse Act - 23
Indian Wars - 21

J
John Iliff - 57
Joseph McCoy - 54
Joseph Smith - 30

L

INDEX

Law and order - 38
Little Crow - 62
Little Crow's War - 63
Loving, Oliver - 56

M

Manifest Destiny - 29
Massacre at Wounded Knee - 81
McCarty, Henry - 74
McCoy, Joseph - 54
Mennonites - 49
Miners - 36
Mormons - 31
Murphy - 76

N

Native Americans - 17
Native Americans - buffalo - 20
Native Americans - horses - 19
Native Americans - tipi - 21

O

Oklahoma Land Rush - 73
Oliver Loving - 56
Oregon Trail - 26

P

Pacific Railroad Act, 1862 - 44
Parker, Ely S - 61
Peace Policy - 61
Permanent Indian Frontier - 22
Pioneer farmers - 25
Plains Indians - 17

Q

Quarantine laws for cattle - 54

R

Railroad companies - 45
Ranch - 59
Red Cloud - 67
Red Cloud's War - 66
Red Turkey - 49
Reno Gang - 52

Reservations - 24

S

San Francisco - 37
Sand Creek Massacre - 65
Scalp - 34
Second Fort Laramie Treaty, 1868 - 69
Second Indian Appropriations Act, 1871 - 62
Seed drill - 70
Settlements on the Plains in 1850s - 33
Sharecroppers - 74
Singleton, Benjamin - 72
Sioux, Dakota - 62
Sitting Bull - 68
Smith, Joseph - 30
Smith, Thomas - 51
Sulky Plow - 48

T

Texas fever - 53
Thomas Smith - 51
Timber and Culture Act, 1873 - 49
Tipi - 21
Trail of Tears - 23
Trail, Chisholm - 55
Trail, Goodnight-Loving - 55
Transcontinental Railroad - 42

V

Vigilantes - 39

W

WSGA - 79
War, Johnson County - 77
War, Lincoln County - 75
Watson, Ella - 78
Whitman, Marcus - 27
Wild Bill Hickok - 52
Windmill - 47
Wounded Knee Massacre - 81
Wyoming Stock Growers Association - 79

Y

Young, Brigham - 33

www.ingramcontent.com/pod-product-compliance
Lightning Source LLC
Chambersburg PA
CBHW050718090526
44588CB00014B/2329